When the White Pine Was King

WHEN THE
WHITE PINE
WAS KING

A History of Lumberjacks, Log Drives, and Sawdust Cities in Wisconsin

JERRY APPS

WISCONSIN HISTORICAL SOCIETY PRESS

Published by the Wisconsin Historical Society Press
Publishers since 1855

The Wisconsin Historical Society helps people connect to the past by
collecting, preserving, and sharing stories. Founded in 1846, the Society
is one of the nation's finest historical institutions.

Join the Wisconsin Historical Society: wisconsinhistory.org/membership

Publication of this book was made possible in part by a grant from the Alice E. Smith fellow-
ship fund.

Front cover image: © John Boettcher, used with permission

Pages ii–iii image: A log-driving crew for the Chippewa Lumber and Boom Company
breaks up a jam, 1895; WHi Image ID 1895

Back cover image of a Northwoods logging crew from Connor Lumber and Land
Company Records, 1872–1982; WHi Image ID 77338

Printed in Canada
Designed by Percolator Graphic Design

24 23 22   3 4 5

Library of Congress Cataloging-in-Publication Data

Names: Apps, Jerold W., 1934– author.
Title: When the white pine was king : a history of lumberjacks, log drives,
    and sawdust cities in Wisconsin / Jerry Apps.
Description: Madison, WI : Wisconsin Historical Society Press, [2020] |
    Includes bibliographical references and index.
Identifiers: LCCN 2020001652 (print) | LCCN 2020001653 (ebook) |
    ISBN 9780870209345 (paperback) | ISBN 9780870209352 (ebook)
Subjects: LCSH: Logging—Wisconsin. | Loggers—Wisconsin.
Classification: LCC HD9757.W5 A67 2020 (print) | LCC HD9757.W5 (ebook) |
    DDC 338.1/749809775—dc23
LC record available at https://lccn.loc.gov/2020001652
LC ebook record available at https://lccn.loc.gov/2020001653

CONTENTS

INTRODUCTION

I grew up in central Wisconsin hearing lumberjack tales. My Grandfather Apps had been a cook in a lumber camp long before my time, and my family passed along some of his stories. We had twenty acres of woodlot on our farm, mostly oaks, but no giant white pines like the ones I heard had once covered the northern regions of the state. I was fascinated, and I wanted to learn more.

I was introduced to axes and crosscut saws—the lumberjack's essential tools—as I helped my dad cut firewood for the woodstoves that heated our drafty farmhouse in winter. We spent considerable time every fall making wood: cutting down dead oaks with axes and two-man crosscut saws, then dragging the logs with our team of horses to the farmstead, where we piled them to await the sawing bee.

On a late-autumn Saturday, Pa would invite neighbors to stop by for a few hours of wood sawing. A half dozen or so men would come by. Guy York brought his circle saw, powered by an old Buick engine and designed primarily for slicing oak logs into blocks that would later be split. The big saw screamed as York fed it each hunk of oak wood; it spewed out a ribbon of sawdust that gathered at his feet. Four other men, usually working in teams of two, carried logs and limbs to the saw. Another man tossed the cut pieces onto an ever-larger pile. When the pile was deemed large enough, York and the crew moved the saw a few feet farther away. Sawing continued, and another wood pile was built. (In the language of the day, each pile of cut wood was referred to as a *set*, referring to how many times the saw had been set up, moved, and set up again. When someone asked the size of his woodpile—as folks in our neighborhood were apt to do—a farmer might reply "four sets" or "five sets.")

We also occasionally cut oak trees for lumber to be used on the farm. We hauled the oak logs to a sawmill in Wild Rose owned and operated by Ernest Knoke. He sawed the logs into two-inch planks that we made into a stone boat to use for removing stones from our rocky farm fields. During World War II, Knoke's sawmill became one of Wild Rose's major employers. I enjoyed visiting the sawmill and hearing the scream of the

I've always enjoyed stories and images of lumberjacks, like this one taken by photographer Charles Van Schaick of Black River Falls over a hundred years ago.
WHI IMAGE ID 92880

enormous circle saw as it sliced its way through oak logs. The sawyer rode on a carriage that moved the log against the saw, and when the saw reached the end of the log, the carriage shot back on its rails before making another cut. It was a loud but fantastic event. During the 1940s and 1950s, Knoke bought marketable timber, mostly oak, from nearby farms. He would send a crew of men with axes and chainsaws and logging trucks to the farms where the logs were cut. They hauled the logs to his mill to be cut into railroad ties, which were in high demand, especially during the war years.

When Waushara County organized a 4-H club in our community, I signed up for the club's forestry project. I received a little booklet that included descriptions of the various species of trees that grow in Wisconsin, from the giant oaks I was familiar with in our woodlot to the aspen trees that Pa called "popple." I learned how to identify trees by inspecting their leaves and needle clusters and to recognize them in all seasons of the year, even in winter, when hardwoods have no leaves.

As a 4-H forestry project member, I received, at no charge, fifty tiny pine seedlings that I planted in a transplant bed. I grew them there for a couple of years and then replanted them on the north side of our woodlot. Today those trees stand seventy-five feet tall and taller. I proudly show them to my grandchildren when we drive by.

One summer in the late 1940s, our forestry group members visited a working logging camp on the Menominee Indian reservation. We talked with the lumberjacks, ate lunch with them in their cook shanty, and visited the sawmill at Neopit. I found the logging and sawmill operation impressive, and I was captivated by the magnificent white pines that grew on the reservation. The reservation land had been spared from the clear-cutting of nearly all white pine across the rest of northern Wisconsin, and the Menominee were following sustainable forestry practices, meaning that they selectively cut trees and replanted for future harvests.

My fascination with trees and forests continued into adulthood. Since 1966, my family has established a tree farm on our land in Waushara County. We have planted at least fifty pine trees every year that we have owned the place; one year we planted seventy-five hundred trees (with the help of a mechanical tree planter). Five years ago, I purchased sixty

A postcard view of the Menominee Indian Reservation's sawmill at Neopit.
WHI IMAGE ID 84544

additional acres of mostly hardwood forest adjacent to our farm, and today we have about one hundred acres of trees, half of them white and red pine and half hardwoods: white oak, black oak, bur oak, maple, birch, black cherry, and poplar. With the help of the Wisconsin Forest Management Program and a professional forester, we practice selective thinning and logging with the hope that my grandchildren and their grandchildren will be able to enjoy our Roshara for years to come.

I also hope our family's future generations will share my interest in our state's logging and lumber history. This book tells those stories—stories of a rugged life in primitive logging camps where lumberjacks worked from dawn to dark cutting down monster trees; stories of river drivers and sawmill operators and entrepreneurs; stories about how logging, lumber, and an assortment of related businesses fueled the growth of our state and continues to shape our lives, our economy, and our culture today. As historian Robert F. Fries noted, "Wood remained of all the gifts of nature the most characteristically American. One may say that the nation has been carved from wood."[1]

Red pine plantation at Roshara. PHOTO © STEVE APPS

1

BEFORE THE LOGGERS ARRIVED

As recently as twenty-five thousand years ago, glaciers still engulfed all but the southwestern corner of what would become Wisconsin. When the great ice sheets had finally melted and retreated to the north, about ten thousand years ago, they left what historian Mark Wyman has described as "two Wisconsins": a cooler northern region and a warmer southern region. The two regions overlapped in central and western Wisconsin, creating what is known as a biological tension zone, where southern and northern plants and animals mingle.[1]

The glaciers also left behind rich deposits that became fertile soil. Grasses were the first plants to grow on the once-glaciated land, but as the climate warmed and soils developed, trees began to take hold. Larch and spruce were the first tree species to arrive in central and northern Wisconsin; next were jack pine, red pine, and balsam fir, followed by deciduous trees. White pine (*Pinus strobus*) was one of the last to appear, arriving eight thousand to nine thousand years ago. Eventually, a vast region of forestland covered the northern two-thirds of what would be Wisconsin, with white pines comprising 30 percent of it. Geographer Mary Dopp described the location of the forested region this way: "If a line was drawn from Manitowoc to Portage, and from there to the falls of the St. Croix, nearly all the forest region proper of the state would be north and the prairies and oak openings south of it."[2]

According to the origin stories of many Wisconsin Indian nations, people have been in the Great Lakes region since time began.

Euro-American archaeologists and other scholars date the first human occupation of this land to around twelve thousand years ago. Descendants of the Upper Paleolithic people, they lived along the glacial margin as the ice moved northward, hunting and gathering food across a wide territory and making their camps at the junctures of rivers.[3] As new species of flora developed, early peoples used those trees and plants in a variety of ways. Some, for example, made flour from the white pine cambium, or inner bark. The white pine also appeared in the storytelling and spiritual traditions of many early peoples; to the Algonquian tribes, the pine represents wisdom, while to the Iroquois, it is a symbol of peace.[4]

Slowly, some early peoples, such as the Oneota, moved from hunting and fishing to farming and established more permanent villages. Beginning around 1000 ce, the Oneota began growing corn, beans, and squash in gardens. They developed a vast trade network with other Native peoples extending as far east as the Atlantic Ocean and as far south as the Gulf of Mexico.[5] Numbering from sixty thousand to seventy thousand by the 1400s, the Oneota made considerable alterations to Wisconsin's landscape in some places, often using fire to manage natural resources. They burned large forest areas to divert big game into smaller, unburned areas where the animals could more easily be hunted, to remove undergrowth in wooded areas and clear paths for easier travel, and to promote or improve certain plants. They gathered willow to make baskets and hazelnuts as a food source.[6]

By the time the first European explorers and emissaries began arriving in the region in the 1630s, the land that would become Wisconsin had long been home to many American Indian nations. They hunted and fished, gathered berries and nuts, collecting maple sap to make sugar, and preserving foods for use in the winter. Most lived in wigwams made from bent tree saplings covered in bark. Communities in the southern and central parts of the state, such as the Menominee and Ho-Chunk, took advantage of the longer growing season to plant gardens; those in the north, such as the Ojibwe, relied less on farming and therefore lived in smaller groups that could travel more easily.[7]

The French were the first Europeans to arrive on this land, and by the late 1600s, France had established an active interest in the region, doing

FACING: An enormous white pine in the town of Ross, Forest County. WHI IMAGE ID 127797

missionary work and trading European goods with Native people for fur pelts, mainly beaver. The Fox–Wisconsin River route from Green Bay to Prairie du Chien had long been a major transport route for the region's inhabitants; now it helped transform Wisconsin into a major fur-trading center.[8]

But trade and a growing economy inevitably brought conflict, and by the 1750s, the French and British were battling for control of the fur trade and the allegiance of the American Indian suppliers. The result, noted Erika Janik in *A Short History of Wisconsin*, was "clandestine attacks, retribution, open warfare, and a tangle of shifting alliances" among the French, English, and tribal nations.[9] Yet throughout that time of great change for the people living here, the landscape of the region overall remained little altered—aside from the utter depletion of the beaver population. A significant transformation of Wisconsin's physical appearance would not take hold until a hundred years later, with the arrival of logging crews in the north.

By the 1830s, white settlers—first Yankees from New England, followed by immigrants from an assortment of European countries, particularly Germany and Norway—began arriving in the region. They settled primarily in southeastern Wisconsin, east and south of the Fox–Wisconsin waterway (although some were drawn to the southwestern lead-mining district), and they set about altering the landscape for their use, establishing small farms where they would attempt to scrape out a living. Much of the land they settled was forested, covered with oaks and maples; the new arrivals cleared the land for farming, using the wood to build houses and other buildings, to make tools and furniture, and to heat their dwellings.[10]

But despite their utility for those basic necessities, the vast acres of hardwoods were often considered a nuisance.[11] Some settlers organized land-clearing bees to help them ready the land for farming. They cut down giant hardwood trees, many of them three hundred years old or older, and heaped them into huge piles to be burned. The smell of oak smoke and the sight of smoldering fires on newly cleared land was common during the early years of southern Wisconsin settlement. Fredericka Bremer, a Swede who toured southern Wisconsin in 1850, described the landscape near

This engraving captured the harsh realities of the lives of early settlers on the Wisconsin frontier. ILLUSTRATION FROM A WISCONSIN STATE BOARD OF IMMIGRATION PAMPHLET, CIRCA 1880

Madison in a letter home, observing, "The trees were not lofty, and the green sward under them as free from underwood as if it had been carefully uprooted. This is attributed to the practice of the Indians to kindle fires year after year upon these grass-grown fields, whereby the bushes and trees were destroyed."[12]

While settlers in southern Wisconsin worked diligently to rid their potential farmland of timber, thousands of acres of pine forests remained in the north, for at the time Wisconsin became a territory, these central and northern Wisconsin regions were American Indian lands. In September 1836, the Menominee Indian nation signed the Treaty of the Cedars (also referred to as the Lumberman's Treaty), ceding most of their land, including a forty-eight-mile strip along the Wisconsin River, to the United States. And in 1837, the US government ratified treaties with the Ho-Chunk, Ojibwe, and Sioux nations, opening up an immense area east of the Mississippi River to exploitation by whites.[13]

Even before the treaties were in place, beginning in 1832 the federal government sent surveyors to the Michigan and Wisconsin Territories to divide the land into 640-acre sections for sale. While that work was still being done, squatters began staking claims. Soon after the treaties were signed, the Wisconsin Territory's US district attorney reported in Washington that "men of enterprise but generally without money" were looking to Wisconsin lands to begin logging and milling operations. In 1837, Gilbert Conant and Daniel Campbell built a dam and sawmill at a Wisconsin River site they named Conant's Rapids. James Harper and Robert Bloomer built a sawmill in 1839 on the Plover River.[14] As many as fifteen small companies employing up to twenty-five men each began operations in the region before it had been surveyed and offered for sale.[15]

While early settlers in Wisconsin were busy planting and harvesting crops, mainly wheat, elsewhere the demand for building materials, primarily pine lumber, was growing. The rapidly expanding populations of towns and cities across the region required lumber for buildings and other structures. And as thousands of settlers moved west of the Mississippi River to the Great Plains, where few trees of any kind were to be found, the demand for pine lumber soared.

The stage was set for a logging boom that would stretch across northern Minnesota, Wisconsin, and Michigan—a vast region that appeared to offer an endless supply of timber. Wisconsin congressman Ben Eastman informed his fellow representatives in Washington in 1852 that Wisconsin's pine forests were "sufficient to supply all the wants of citizens . . . for all time to come."[16]

2

THE LOGGING BOOM

White pine quickly became the favored wood for America's building boom. The wood is soft but tough, with a straight grain, and it is easy to work with a hand saw, a drawshave, and a wood chisel—making it the nearly perfect material for rafters and joists, framing, siding, flooring, and shingles. As one chronicler of the state's timber industry described the pine's qualities: "It holds paints and glues well and is the cabinetmakers and woodworkers delight, for it can be quickly fashioned into almost any desired form. . . . When fresh from the planing mill the boards are as smooth as velvet and have a beautiful pearly sheen."[1] One of pine's most noteworthy characteristics is that it floats in water, which made it possible to transport the massive logs down Wisconsin's major rivers to sawmills to be cut for lumber, lath, and other products.

Thanks to a highly favorable climate and soil conditions, Wisconsin's white pine proved superior to that grown in the neighboring states. Wisconsin white pines grow to a height of more than seventy-five feet in fifty years and can eventually reach a height of 120 feet and diameter of more than thirty inches. It is not uncommon for white pine trees to live two hundred years or longer.[2] By the early 1800s, Wisconsin's pine forests had as many as sixteen to twenty mature trees per acre, yielding as much as forty thousand board feet per acre. (A board foot is twelve inches by twelve inches by one inch.) In less favorable parts of the Northwoods, the yield might be only one thousand to three thousand board feet per acre.[3]

The first lumber speculators to arrive in the region saw the advantages available here—millions of acres of virgin pine, rivers to transport the logs, and waterpower to drive sawmills—and envisioned an economic empire.

A crew sorts pine logs on the Peshtigo River, 1900. WHI IMAGE ID 2884

One of the first was Pennsylvania-born Franklin Steele, an early settler of Minneapolis, who in 1838 joined with some associates to organize the St. Croix Falls Lumber Company and embarked on the first attempt to produce lumber in the St. Croix Valley.[4]

Yet, despite the abundance of timber and waterpower, the industry was slow at first to proliferate, due in part to a lack of skilled workers. Most locals had no experience in the technical side of the work, which required cutting timber in a wilderness area, transporting the logs to sawmills, and building and operating those mills, which were larger and more complicated than the small pioneer sawmills then found in the southern regions of the state. Lumbermen in New England and eastern Canada had more years of experience with lumber production, and Wisconsin entrepreneurs began recruiting men from New Brunswick, Maine, New Hampshire, New York, and Pennsylvania to bring their expertise to the Wisconsin pinery. The Wisconsin speculators ran paid advertisements in eastern newspapers that "described in glowing terms the present prosperity of the territory, the potentialities of lumbering, and the vast amount of government land available at a nominal price."[5] Early recruits from the East who made a

name for themselves in Wisconsin include Philetus Sawyer (from Ver-
mont, later a US senator), Isaac Stephenson (New Brunswick and Maine),
the Doughty brothers (New Brunswick), and Orrin H. Ingram (Massachusetts and New York).[6]

Wisconsin's logging industry experienced its first round of boom years
from 1850 to 1856. The Wisconsin census of 1840 reported that lumber
produced in the state in that year was worth $202,239; by 1850, the value of
Wisconsin's lumber had reached $1,218,506. The industry slowed after the
Economic Panic of 1857 but by 1860 was once again booming, with a value
that year of $4,377,880. Wisconsin's wheat production was at its peak in the
1860s, and prosperous farmers bought lumber to add buildings and make
other improvements on their farms. More newcomers arrived after the
Homestead Act of 1862 made 160 acres of federally owned land available
to settlers at no charge other than a ten-dollar fee, the only requirements
being that the farmer had to live on the property for five years and make
improvements—which included buildings—in that time.[7]

The market for lumber outside Wisconsin was also increasing in the
1850s and 1860s. The rapidly growing big cities of the Midwest, such as
Chicago and St. Louis, were a major market. In 1864, the price of lumber
was at an unprecedented twenty-three dollars per one thousand board feet
in the Chicago market.[8] And with the expansion of railroads and water
shipping, a market for Wisconsin lumber grew in the East as well.

As the Civil War raged, the need for lumber from Wisconsin's pineries
had never been higher. Federal contracts like the one Daniel Shaw and
Company of Eau Claire had with the US Army amounted to an annual
average of 1.5 million board feet of lumber purchased during the first three
years of the war. The Shaw company saw an order of 3 million board feet
in 1865, the last year of the war.[9]

Even as war-induced labor shortages slowed production in both the
woods and the mills, rising prices and demand served the lumber industry well. By 1866, Wisconsin's lumber companies were cutting some
800 million board feet of lumber a year. By 1869, annual lumber output
reached 1.2 billion board feet, and in 1872, the lumber harvest from the
Wisconsin Northwoods reached 1.6 billion board feet, a record that held
for nine years.[10] In 1870, the value of lumber produced in the state was
$15,130,719. In 1880, it reached $17,952,347, and in 1890, an unbelievable

$60,966,444 worth of lumber was harvested from Wisconsin's North-woods.[11] The 1890 US census recorded more than twenty-three thousand men working in logging operations and thirty-two thousand in sawmills. Logging and lumber businesses employed one-quarter of Wisconsin workers in that decade.[12]

In 1861, "to regulate the traffic in logs, timber, and lumber," the Wisconsin legislature formally divided Wisconsin's northwestern Northwoods into lumber districts: the Wisconsin River and its tributaries, the Black River and its tributaries, the Chippewa River and its tributaries, and the St. Croix River and its tributaries.[13] In 1863, the legislature added a Green Bay district; others followed in later years. Each district was assigned a lumber inspector to enforce regulations and settle disputes related to log ownership.[14]

The districts did not share equally in the wealth. The Wisconsin district garnered the least of the lumber wealth at the time because the Wisconsin River, with its many twists and turns and dangerous waterfalls, made transporting logs difficult and expensive. The Chippewa region produced the most wealth; its pine forests were plentiful, and the Chippewa River flowed well, with few rapids or sharp turns. Economist Frederick Merk wrote of the Chippewa region, "One-sixth of all the white pine to be found in the United States was said to be standing within its confines."[15]

COMMERCIAL SAWMILLS

Where some entrepreneurs saw opportunity in harvesting Wisconsin's pine forests, others sought their fortune in cutting that harvest into lumber. (Of course, many invested in both.) The first sawmills on the frontier, though, were established for local use by settlers eager to replace hastily constructed sod huts and log cabins and barns with frame buildings. In 1794, Jacob Franks bought land from Menominee Indians near present-day De Pere; the sawmill he built there was by some recollections the first in "the whole 'Northwest Territory.'"[16]

According to geographer Mary Dopp, commercial lumber production in Wisconsin began in 1809 when another sawmill was built near De Pere. Another was built in 1816 to supply lumber for the fort at Green Bay.[17] In 1831, Daniel Whitney built the first commercial sawmill on the Wiscon-

Daniel Whitney's map of the Brown County village of Navarino, at the mouth of the Fox River. WHI IMAGE ID 69323

sin River at Whitney Rapids, across the river from present-day Nekoosa. Whitney had obtained both the permission of the Menominee Indians and approval by the US War Department, as at that time the lands along the Wisconsin River from the Fox–Wisconsin portage northward were Menominee Indian territory. Amable Grignon II and his partner, Morgan L. Martin, also received a permit to build a sawmill in Menominee territory, which they did in about 1837.[18]

On the western edge of what would become Wisconsin, the first sawmill and logging enterprise began in 1828. Its history was recalled in a 1916 Eau Claire newspaper article:

In the spring of 1828, James H. Lockwood, afterwards better known as Judge Lockwood, an Indian fur trader, and General Street, of the United States Army, Indian agent at Fort Crawford, obtained a permit from the great chief Wabashaw of Wabashaw's band of Sioux Indians, and also from the chiefs of the Chippewa band that claimed the lands on the Chippewa and Red Cedar, now Menomonie River, to cut pine timber, to occupy a certain tract of land and to build a sawmill thereon, in consideration of certain articles of merchandise, blankets, beads, whiskey, etc. to be paid annually in July to the former at Wabashaw's Prairie, now Winona, and to the latter at the mill to be built on the land leased. The sanction of government was also obtained, and under this arrangement, the aforementioned parties above fitted out an expedition and erected a sawmill on Wilson's Creek, a short distance from its confluence with the Red Cedar. This was the first mill built in the Chippewa Valley, and its site is now the west side center of the village of Menomonie.[19]

Even as sawmill operations became larger and more commercial and operators were able to modernize their equipment, the basic operation of a sawmill remained mostly unchanged. The building housing the saw equipment resembled a barn and included beams, belts, saws—and sawdust flying everywhere. In the early days, the saw was a single blade (a muley saw) that moved up and down; next came mills with several up-and-down blades. By the mid-1850s, mills were using large rotary blades; by the 1890s, nearly all used band saws. Mills began using turbines as their power source by the 1850s; by the 1870s, many were powered by steam engines, which generally had a refuse burner with a tall smokestack to carry the smoke away from the boilers that created the steam for the steam engine.[20] (For more on the steam revolution in sawmill operations, see page 105.)

The first commercial sawmills were located on water resources in the heart of timber holdings. But if the nearby river posed challenges—rapids or tight turns, for instance—that made transporting logs to the mill difficult, the owner would be more likely to build at a central location farther from where the logs were cut to minimize the water transport required. The Wisconsin River was one of the most challenging ones for log driving, and therefore many cities close to its banks, such as Wausau and Stevens Point, became sites of early commercial sawmills. By 1849, forty-seven sawmills were located along the Wisconsin River, with some fifteen hundred to two thousand men employed to raft logs and lumber. By the mid-1870s, seven logging companies—the R. Connor Company in Stratford, R. Connor Company in Auburndale, John Weeks Lumber Company in Stevens Point, Grand Rapids Lumber Company in Wisconsin Rapids,

Early Wisconsin sawmill workers (note the exposed blade). WHI IMAGE ID 91823

McMillan Lumber Company in McMillan, Stoddard Lumber Company in Stevens Point, and Joseph Dessert Company in Mosinee—were sending logs to forty-seven sawmills on the upper Wisconsin.[21]

On rivers where log driving was easier, such as the Wolf, Black, Chippewa, and St. Croix, sawmills could be built farther downriver from the pine forests, and by 1850, thriving sawmills had been established at Oshkosh, La Crosse, Eau Claire, and Chippewa Falls. The city of Eau Claire was known to receive logs from as far away as fifty miles from Lake Superior.[22]

Sawmills emerged in other parts of the state as well. John P. Arndt built a small water-powered mill on Menominee land at Duck Creek in 1827; he opened the first sawmill in Oconto County in 1829.[23] After David Davidson built a sawmill in 1853 at what would become Suamico, a village emerged around the mill, including some fifteen houses, a blacksmith shop, and various barns and sheds. Neil Munro, a friend of Davidson's, built a second mill there a few years later. In one history of Suamico, the unnamed author wrote, "As soon as the mills were running, workers came from many countries to settle where there was work to be had. Surveyors came and cruised the forest for fine stands of timber to be bought by the mills. Ox teams hauled the lumber out of the woods and to the mills where it was sawed. This region was noted for shaved and later sawed shingles, which were made by hand. The shingles were hauled to the Green Bay market by ox team. Supplies were brought to the mill sites on the return trip."[24]

The growth and entrepreneurship spurred by Suamico's first mills is a story repeated in many Wisconsin sawmill towns. Following the successes of Davidson and Munro, M. E. Tremble and partners bought an existing mill at the mouth of the Little Suamico River in 1870; after a few months, Tremble bought out his partners. He also purchased large tracts of pineland to supply his mills, which proved profitable, and he built a boarding house, several small houses, and a store. To aid in the shipment of his lumber products, Tremble improved the village's dock and straightened the river's channel so boats could come up the river. And to the surprise of many, he oversaw the building of a three-masted sailing vessel named the *M. E. Tremble*, which was launched on August 15, 1875. Several other ships carried on a steady business between Suamico and Milwaukee, Racine, and Chicago, carrying lumber products to those markets.[25]

A Wood Products Boom

Wisconsin's logging and lumber boom provided a seemingly endless supply of materials that would spawn dozens of innovative wood products businesses, many of them based in cities situated near waterways that could be used both for power and transport. As those operations became established, they in turn fueled continued growth of the lumber industry.

For example, La Crosse, strategically located where the Black and La Crosse Rivers flow into the Mississippi, established its first sawmill in 1852; by 1855, the city counted a pail factory, a plow factory, and a machine shop among its business enterprises. A wooden pail maker founded in Menasha in 1849 would go on to become a leader in the manufacture of assorted wooden products, including barrel staves, broom handles, clothespins, and containers; by 1915, the company was known as Menasha Woodenware and consumed more than 150,000 acres of timberland annually.[26] Eau Claire, too, became home to a host of wood-related business, which by the 1880s included nine sawmills; a pulp and paper mill; a wooden trunk factory; three window, sash, and door plants; seven planing mills; a barrel and stave factory; two breweries; and three carriage and wagon factories.[27]

In addition to producing sawn lumber, mills began producing shingles to cover the thousands of roofs being constructed across the region. The first farmers in the region made shingles by hand, and by the start

THE TANNING INDUSTRY

When Wisconsin's lumber industry was at its peak, the white pine was the lumberman's tree of choice. Hemlock was dismissed, and at first largely spared, because its quality as a building material was far inferior to that of pine.

As pioneers flooded into the Midwest and then farther west, demand grew for a number of materials, not just lumber. As historian John Bates related, these new settlers "required vast stores of clothing, as well as horse harnesses, saddles, reins and an enormous array of other leather goods."[1] A leather-tanning industry quickly emerged—and it relied on the bark of the hemlock, which contained tannic acid to aid in the process of converting animal hides into leather.

Lumbermen cut hemlock trees during May, June, and July. Using a tool called a draw shave, boys too young to work in the woods peeled the bark from the trees, usually leaving the rest of the tree to rot. The bark slabs were cured, stacked, "and left until late fall when they were hauled by wagon, sailing sloop, or train to the tanneries."[2]

Employees of the N. R. Allen Tannery of Kenosha, 1918. WHI IMAGE ID 120071

(continued)

Wisconsin's tanneries were concentrated in the Lake Michigan port cities of Kenosha, Racine, Sheboygan, Milwaukee, Two Rivers, and Green Bay; according to Bates, "Turn-of-the-twentieth-century Milwaukee produced more income from tanning hides than from making beer."[3] Inland tanneries could also be found in Medford, Rib Lake, Phillips, Prentice, and Mellen. But by the late 1800s, the tanning industry replaced hemlock bark with chromium salts in the tanning process, and hemlock trees were once again spared.

Notes
1. John Bates, " 'The World Walked on Milwaukee Leather': Hemlock and Wisconsin's Tanning Industry," *Wisconsin Magazine of History* 101, no. 8 (Summer 2018): 43–49.
2. Bates, 43–49.
3. Bates, 43–49.

of the Civil War, Wisconsin farm families were producing an estimated 175 million shingles annually.[28] But as Wisconsin's workforce, including its farmers, headed off to the war, demand quickly grew for machine-sawed shingles—despite their inferior quality compared to those that were hand-shaved. From 1860 to 1870, shingle mills developed more quickly than sawmills in Wisconsin, and by 1870, Wisconsin led the nation in the production of wooden shingles. In 1869, Wisconsin produced 806,800,000 shingles, half of them manufactured in the Green Bay area.[29]

In 1852, four mills were operating in Oshkosh. By 1866, that number had increased to fifty mills producing 8 million shingles, 14 million lath, and 85 million feet of lumber.[30] Woodworking would reign as a leading industry in Oshkosh for several decades.

Wisconsin's abundant pine forests served as an engine of the state's economic growth in myriad ways throughout the 1800s. The mighty white pine was a catalyst for other iconic industries that are woven indelibly throughout Wisconsin's culture and economy, such as wood products manufacturing, papermaking, and printing. None of it would have been possible without the early logging and lumber companies and their thousands of workers employed to harvest the trees, move the logs, and cut the lumber for market.

John Strange's Pail & Tub Factory, Menasha. WHI IMAGE ID 39180

Shingle mill workers at the Scott and Taylor Lumber Company, Ashland, circa 1895.
WHI IMAGE ID 57657

3

SETTING UP CAMP
AND CREW

As federal land surveyors completed their work in 1866, the US government made much of the surveyed land available for sale. In addition, in 1862, Congress passed the Morrill Act, granting blocks of federal lands to states, which could in turn use or sell the land to establish agriculture and engineering colleges. Wisconsin gained ownership of 240,000 acres of land, and the state legislature designated any resulting proceeds to the University of Wisconsin.[1] All of these lands were available for logging companies and speculators to purchase.

In the late 1880s, the average price of good pineland on the open market was between $2.50 and $5.00 per acre, yet logging companies buying state-owned land paid as little as $1.00 per acre, sometimes less. With such low prices, by 1871 the acreage of state-owned lands in Wisconsin dropped to about half of what it was in the mid-1860s, and by 1883, Wisconsin had only one million acres remaining of the five million the state originally owned through a series of federal land grants.[2]

The large lumber companies, such as Stephenson, Sawyer, and Weyerhauser, owned many thousands of acres of pineland in northern Wisconsin. The Menominee River Lumber Company, for example, owned seventy-five thousand acres of pineland; Weyerhauser holdings were even greater. By 1913, ten owners held 24 percent of all the pineland in Wisconsin.[3]

FACING: A page from the 1881 diary of timber cruiser John H. Goddard. WHI IMAGE ID 121196

TIMBER CRUISERS

Even with such attractive prices for land, before a logging company would sign on the dotted line it sent a timber cruiser, sometimes known as a *land-looker*, to inspect the land and assess its timber potential. Timber cruisers were sometimes employed by the lumber company, but they often worked as independent contractors. Timber cruisers usually had other experience in the industry, such as supervising a logging crew or scaling lumber (measuring board feet). Working alone or in small groups, the cruisers traveled overland or by river into the area to be cruised and then established a base camp where they would sleep in tents and do their cooking.

The timber cruiser next calculated the amount of desirable lumber on the land available for purchase. To estimate the number of trees and their board feet, the cruiser paced off an area two hundred feet square, or approximately one acre. He then counted the number of trees in the marked

5-4

Thursday Feb 2nd Were up early and after breakfast packed the tetangans had both of them well loaded having about one hundred pounds on each of them Mr Dundass told us where we would find the trail Joe and I took the lead with one load Clark followed with the other we followed the logging road about two miles to the north and west and then started through the swamp we had to cut the brush ahead for the tetangans to pass in about half a mile from the road we came to a small lake and it was snowing hard while we crossed it, took dinner by the lake side and then went up quite a hill through a tamarac and spruce swamp across another lake, through more swamp and hemlock and we came to the trail it was 4.20 P.M. when we reached it and we went about half a mile over

5-5-

it before camping, it was well beaten but so many short crooks that it bothered the tetangans when we camped we were about two miles farther west than Dundass camp

Friday Feb 3rd took the trail to the east for nearly an hour we were going up hill all the time the ground was very rough but covered with hard wood this was a part of Pinoka iron range toward night we found where the compass would not work very well the north end of the needle drawing toward the ground went into camp about four P.M. for we did not sleep much the night before and we wanted time to cook before dark

Saturday 4th continued our way to the east about 10.30 A.M arrived at Sylies fork of Bad river there was a fall of about eight feet here, across the river was a small shanty built for the packers on the trail

area. He scaled several of the trees to determine an average number of board feet per tree. Then he multiplied the number of trees in the marked-off acre by the average board feet per tree to arrive at the approximate board feet of lumber that acre would produce. Finally, he multiplied the estimated board feet per acre by the number of acres in a section (640) to estimate the number of board feet in the section. The most experienced cruisers were extremely accurate; some could climb one tall tree on a ridge, giving them a panoramic view of the potential logging area, and estimate the board feet for the entire area.

Many cruisers did their work in winter, preferring frozen ground, deep snow, and frigid temperatures to the misery of being attacked by mosquitoes and black flies. It was also easier to move supplies into the cruiser's camp using a toboggan on snow-covered land or across frozen waterways. Experienced cruisers in the employ of a logging company could earn as much as $3.50 a day while cruising timber, with the company providing supplies and equipment.[4]

Establishing a Logging Camp

When the cruising was completed and the results reported were positive, the logging company purchased the land and chose a site for the logging camp. Martin Page, an early logger in the Chippewa Valley, remembered how his company decided where to build a logging camp: "A 'dugout' or 'canoe' was made out of a large pine log and loaded with provisions and blankets for a several weeks' cruise. We would follow up the streams, noting the timber on either side and unless we could see enough good timber on the two sides of the stream convenient for hauling, for a winter's work we could go on until we did find such a place. This was a pretty established rule."[5]

By the 1860s and 1870s, establishing a logging camp involved sending timber cruisers into the woods to estimate the volume of timber by tree species; acquiring timber rights for the potential logging area; obtaining supplies such as sleds, tools, food for the lumberjacks, and feed for the animals; and transporting everything to the logging camp site. The workforce was hired, about twenty-five men for the average logging camp, and a skeleton crew headed to the prospective camp site. The crew con-

A Wisconsin logging camp photographed by Charles J. Van Schaick of Black River Falls.
WHI IMAGE ID 94170

structed the camp buildings from logs, cut rough roads to allow supplies to be brought in, and did any necessary clearing of trees around the camp. At the beginning of winter, the rest of the crew arrived and the logging operation began.[6]

Like timber cruising, most logging took place during the winter months when the ground was frozen, the mosquitoes were absent, and snow cover provided a means for more efficiently moving logs from the forest to the river banks, where they would remain until the spring breakup of the rivers. Longtime lumberman John Emmett Nelligan recalled how he and a small crew of workers established a camp on the Oconto River about fifty miles northwest of Green Bay: "On the first of November, 1874, we started out on the tote road along the river with a cavalcade of two four-horse teams and two yokes of oxen hauling wagons loaded with the necessary supplies and equipment to open a logging camp in the woods. . . . We arrived at the location . . . the third day out of Oconto and immediately set to work."[7]

Part of the group prepared a temporary shelter for the workers, while others cleared the ground for the more permanent camp buildings. They felled trees suitable for use in constructing a building to serve as bunkhouse, kitchen, and mess hall.[8] Early Wisconsin logging camps were crude affairs. Many were constructed in the style of logging camps of Maine, which had been home to many men who had moved west to work in the Wisconsin pinery. The log bunkhouse was typically about twenty-four feet wide and thirty-six feet long. The sidewalls were only about three logs high. The roof consisted of wood shake shingles and was often covered with hemlock or cedar boughs to keep the heat in. An open fireplace, used for both cooking and heating the space, was positioned in the center of the building and about fifteen feet from the door on an elevated platform. An opening in the roof allowed the smoke to escape and, in most camps, provided the only natural lighting, as there were no windows in bunkhouses before 1870. Other light was provided by kerosene lamps and lanterns.[9]

The workers slept in what was called a field bed on one side of the building, with their heads to the outside wall. The men lay on hemlock boughs or hay and covered themselves with heavy quilts. A long bench called the deacon seat stood at their feet. The opposite side of the room included the water barrel, a grindstone, and a wash sink.[10]

Lumberjacks gather in the bunkhouse at Ole Emerson's logging camp in Bayfield County, circa 1904. WHI IMAGE ID 83371

The nights were long and often miserably cold in a northern Wisconsin winter. The bunkhouse was reasonably warm near the source of heat (a fireplace in early camps, a woodstove in later years), but the interior walls were often covered with frost in the morning. The men who quickly assembled the buildings usually spent little time fitting the logs tightly together. Even when they used moss or mud to chink the open spaces between logs, those materials cracked and failed in below-zero weather.

L. E. Barnum, a former camp cook, described the inside of a bunkhouse this way:

> The room is 20 feet by 32 feet . . . at the right of the door . . . is the barrel of water for washing hands and faces. On shelves above it are two pails of drinking water. Beside it is a long wooden sink for three wash basins. Nearby are three or four roller towels on home-made rollers. Near the center of the room . . . is a large heating stove round with a steam boiler and long enough to take four-foot wood. On top of the stove is a circular galvanized tank that holds ten gallons or more of water, which is always warm for washing hands and faces.
>
> Frame arrangement on both sides of the room are the men's bunks, four double ones on each side. This gives room for thirty-two men to sleep. . . . The bunks are merely wide shelves or platforms made of boards with an eight-inch board around the sides. The lower bunk is about a foot from the floor. The upper one is perhaps five feet high. There is a bench along the front edge of the lower ones, which serves as a seat. The beds are made of hay covered with blankets. A small table at the further end of the room furnishes a place for the usual game of poker each evening. Ventilation is secured by a half window sash in the peak of the roof, which can be opened and closed by means of a long pole. The only light during the daytime is that which enters through this skylight and the two windows beside the door.[11]

Thomas McBean, a one-time lumberjack working in the Chippewa Valley, reported that in the logging camps he knew in the 1850s, "the men slept . . . in bunks . . . built on poles . . . and each covered with hay. There were two in a bunk; each had a pair of blankets and their turkey (a grain sack with extra clothing in it) for a pillow."[12]

In addition to the main building, most early camps included a log building for housing oxen and, later, horses. As the years passed, the rude log hovel used to house a team of oxen or horses was replaced with a stable or, in some instances, a barn. Larger camps that used many horses employed a barn boss, who oversaw the cleaning of the barn and general care of the horses.

According to historian Malcolm Rosholt, after 1875 most logging camps also included a blacksmith shop. Blacksmiths of the day were ingenious in their ability to construct almost anything needed for logging work out of metal or wood. They made cant hooks and peaveys and repaired axes, saws, and sleighs. They were also responsible for shoeing horses.[13]

Economist Frederick Merk described Wisconsin camps this way:

A typical lumber camp in the Wisconsin pineries presented to the spectator a combination of sights and sounds. The rapid tap of the chopper's ax, the sudden crash as here and there a majestic pine thundered to the earth, the intermittent rip of the saw as it rent the fallen giant into logs, the jingle of bells on the ox-drawn sled as it slowly moved off with its load to the river bank, or returned on the run for a new burden of logs, the hearty shouts of the red-shirted lumberjacks as they hastened about their work in the keen and exhilarating winter air, all this was the foreground for which, in strange contrast, the background was the solemn grandeur of the forest.[14]

THE LOGGING CREW

Some of Wisconsin's earliest logging camp workers came from Maine, New Hampshire, and New Brunswick. When those eastern forests were depleted, the men took their valuable experience to the pineries of northern Michigan, Wisconsin, and Minnesota. By the time logging was a well-established industry in Wisconsin, in the mid-1800s, many of the camp workers were farmers who headed to Northwoods logging camps for work during the winter months, leaving their wives and children to tend to things at home.

The lumberjack's life had its rewards. For logging camp workers in the late 1800s, pay ranged from twenty-six to thirty dollars a month, depend-

The crew at D. Sullivan's logging camp near Antigo, Langlade County, 1886.
WHI IMAGE ID 5826

ing on economic conditions, plus board and bunk. River drivers earned up to fifty dollars a month, and cooks received from eighty to one hundred dollars a month.[15] Generally, the food was ample and filling, and there was plenty of camaraderie to be had with fellow workers. On the downside, those men who were married wouldn't see their wives or children until spring—though in some logging camps, workers were able to return home for Christmas.

By the late 1890s, women occasionally worked in logging camps, usually as cooks or assistant cooks. Separate sleeping quarters were provided for them, usually adjacent to the camp kitchen. Frank E. Cummings, who moved with his family from Maine to Wisconsin in the 1860s, began working in a camp when he was thirteen. He recalled in a 1916 article in the *Eau Claire Leader* that his mother had been hired by William Pond to cook in a logging camp near Augusta in Eau Claire County where his stepfather also worked. Cummings reported, "At that time there were a good many women cooks in camps, perhaps for two reasons: First the crews were small as compared to those in later years and second, there were fewer males who had learned the gentle art of cooking."[16]

Some bands of Ojibwe Indians who wintered in the forests south of Lake Superior established their winter camps near a logging camp, and by the 1850s some of them worked in the camps as lumberjacks. A small number of African Americans found work in the camps as well; in 1880, 219 African Americans lived in northern Wisconsin counties, and some of them reported working in camps.[17]

In a 1917 *Eau Claire Leader* article, onetime lumberjack Martin Page described the men he worked with in the Chippewa Valley in the 1850s: "The crew consisted of about twenty men, with three yoke of oxen. The woodsmen were mostly French, Irish and Yankees, many from the lumbering regions of Maine and northern New York. There were very few Scandinavians in the Chippewa Valley at the time, although we had one Norwegian, Peter Tronson, in our camp. . . . There were a few Germans, but as a rule, they did not take to lumbering."[18]

Before the 1860s, the logging crews were often small, usually no more than twenty men. By the late 1800s, some of the logging camps boasted as many as sixty or more workers. No matter its size, a typical logging camp crew included the following positions:

Foreman: The boss of the entire crew. One of the foreman's most challenging tasks was keeping order among the lumberjacks. Living in rustic quarters and working hard all day, men often got into squabbles, many of them minor but some more serious. Sometimes the foreman needed a strong arm to discipline a misbehaving lumberjack. In some camps, if someone broke a camp rule, he was fined. Some foremen introduced religious services on Sunday mornings, hoping to tame some of the more rowdy lumberjacks.

Cook: Planned and prepared all the meals.

Cookee: Assisted the cook, including hauling water and carrying firewood.

Clerk: Operated a small store and tallied the timesheets for the men.

Filer: Sharpened the logging tools.

Blacksmith: Made and repaired tools and shoed the oxen and horses.

Cook and cookee at a camp in Hayward, Sawyer County. WHI IMAGE ID 1962

Teamster: Drove and cared for the oxen and draft horses; hauled the logs to the riverbank.

Swamper: Made and repaired the sled tracks in the woods for the heavily loaded logging sleds, cut away brush for the skidders, and assisted lumberjacks by cutting the limbs from felled trees.

Skidder: Supervised moving the logs from the woods to the riverbanks.

Log scaler: Recorded the quality of logs, noted defects, and measured quantity after the logs were piled on the riverbank awaiting transport to a sawmill.

Lumberjack: Included choppers, who felled the trees, and sawyers, who cut the logs into the appropriate lengths for the sawmills.[19]

Two young Wisconsin lumberjacks. WHI IMAGE ID 106379

Working in the woods on below-zero days required warm clothing. One visitor to the north, upon seeing a group of lumbermen for the first time, described their clothing as "picturesque": "Some of them had red sort of stockings reaching from ankle to knee or thereabouts, more like a gaiter than anything else. All or nearly all had rubbers, the large sort with heels, so that either they had thick stockings on and just drew the rubbers over them, or else they had felt boots and the rubbers over those. . . . The coats the men wear . . . are called 'Mackinaws.' They seem to be made out of colored blankets and have different patterns."[20]

John Ziebarth from the Green Bay area worked in lumber camps in Michigan and in northern Wisconsin starting when he was sixteen. During the years 1899 and 1900, he wrote letters home to his parents and other members of his family. Several of his letters are now the property of Ray Clark, a logging historian living in Sobieski, Wisconsin. Here are two of the letters, with minor corrections.

Mich. 1899 December 17th
Dear Father and Mother,

I got your kind and welcome letter the 1 of Dec. I think you are all expecting a letter. I am getting along alright, and I hope you were the same. We had a big snowstorm Monday and it lasted all day. I have 34 working days in. I don't think of coming down [for] Christmas. I got myself a pair of rubbers. They cost $2.50. They are going to start hauling after new years.

The fellow that used to sleep with me jumped Monday and helped himself to my drawers and a pair of mitts. You need not trouble your self by sending anything down. I will see that I dress with that I got. It aint very cold in the daytime but heavy frost at night. They are going to have two seigen [skidding] teams at work all winter.

I have had no kick [complaint] yet. I like the board and it aint so very hard work. I don't think you will know me in spring for I am gaining very fast. I expect to stay hear till in spring. I think I will close my letter now for I have not much to say. But all I said is to let you know that I am well and I hope you were that same.

When writing me a letter send me the news and tell me if all the rest of the boys is to home. I bid farewell with all my best regards to you all Father and Mother. So goodbye to you all. You need not expect me Christmas for I am going to stay here.

Hick Burns, Blades Camp Menominee Mich.

Armstrong Creek Wis Dec. 2nd 1900

Dear Parents,

I'll answer your kind and welcome letter you wrote me while I was up in Mich. I came down Thursday night with the 11.20 train and I met Uncle Richter stand ahead a Saloon door and asked him where to go first because I didn't know him. And he told me to come with him and stay over night. So it was 12 o'clock when I went to bed and I met Gus and Willie Komosky and went up to the Murphy lumber Co. I like the place alright.

I have $16 left of my big winters stack. I am getting $30 a month for notching and will stay here all winter that is if I can. I will tell you my story in spring about Mich.

So goodbye to you all with my very best regards to you all from your son, John. I am well and take you were the same. Write me the news. My address is John Zebarth, Armstrong Creek Wis Murphy Lumber Co.[21]

4

THE LUMBERJACK'S LIFE

Winter mornings in the Northwoods were dark and cold with temperatures sometimes dipping to thirty-five or forty below zero and the sun not rising until as late as 7:40. Workdays for the cook and cookee began about three in the morning. The cook began making breakfast while the cookee built fires in the kitchen and the bunkhouse. The cookee awakened the teamsters at four. They fed and harnessed the horses. The lumberjacks were awakened about four thirty by the cookee yelling that breakfast was on the table. Soon after breakfast, the teamsters with their horses and the loaders set off for the woods. At first light, the lumberjacks followed, in some cases walking a mile or farther to get to the cutting site.

The logging crew's primary job was cutting down trees, always a difficult and dangerous task. The simple ax was the lumberjack's essential tool. (Trees were felled using only axes until about 1870, when the two-man crosscut saw was introduced, making the job easier and quicker.) The lumberjack began by notching the tree on the side of the trunk toward which he wanted the tree to fall. It took careful "reading" of the tree to determine where it should fall so it would not strike another tree or, worse, hang up in another tree, creating what was known as a widow maker. No one knew when or where a widow maker would fall, a hazardous situation that too often resulted in injury or death.

With the tree notched, lumberjacks at each end of a crosscut saw began sawing the trunk on the side opposite the notch. The massive pine would slowly begin to lean in the desired direction and eventually would begin to crack loudly. One lumberjack would pound a steel wedge into the cut to

Lumberjacks fell a white pine with a crosscut saw. WHI IMAGE ID 2413

prevent the saw blade getting trapped. The workers would step out of the way as the tree finally came down with a crash. Next, sawyers used axes to remove the limbs and then lumberjacks used crosscut saws to saw the downed tree into appropriate lengths, usually sixteen feet but sometimes twelve or fourteen feet, depending on the requirements of the sawmill where the logs were headed.

While the lumberjacks were busy cutting down trees and sawing them into logs for transport, swampers were busy clearing a trail through the woods to one of the logging roads. Oxen moved the logs from stump to river's edge until about 1875, after which time draft horses did the job. The most common way to move logs to the logging road was a little sledlike contraption called a go-devil, usually made by the camp blacksmith. One end of the log was lifted onto the device, and a horse pulled the go-devil through the woods to the logging trail. At the logging trail, a crew of men loaded the logs onto bobsleds pulled by horses to the river's edge, where they were unloaded, piled up, and would remain until the river ice melted in spring and the logs were rolled into the river to float to a sawmill.

Hauling piles of logs on a sled pulled by a team on an icy logging road was dangerous, even more so when the roads were hilly. Teamsters struggled to keep control of the team and the load, especially on steep downgrades where there was always the risk of a runaway sled. Some crews had a worker called a road monkey, or monkey man, who covered the icy road with sand or hay before the day's work began.[1]

A team of horses pull a go-devil in Marathon County, 1910. WHI IMAGE ID 58515

A horse-drawn sled carries a large load of logs. WHI IMAGE ID 77661

FOREST FIRES

To add to the risks of the lumberjack's trade, fire was a regular threat throughout the Northwoods during the logging era, especially in dry years. Fires in 1863, 1864, 1868, 1871, 1880, 1891, 1894, 1897, 1908, 1910, 1923, 1931, and 1933 destroyed thousands of acres of valuable timberland.[1]

The year 1864 was an especially bad one for forest fires. It had been a dry spring, and by mid-May, fires were advancing through the timberland on the upper Wisconsin and Black Rivers. Residents of Wausau, Two Rivers, and Neillsville fought valiantly against the flames. Hundreds of acres of timber were lost. Four years later, in 1868, fires again marched through the pineries along the Chippewa, Black, Wisconsin, and Wolf Rivers; the forests of Kewaunee and Door Counties also suffered severe losses.[2]

In a 1917 article, lumberjack John L. Bracklin related his experience in a Sawyer County fire in 1898. That fall had been exceedingly dry in Wisconsin's Northwoods, and Bracklin's father, James Bracklin, a superintendent of logging and log driving for the Knapp, Stout, and Company lumber operation, asked his son to travel to one of the company's more remote camps to make some preparations.

At the camp, John and two other men hooked two yoke of oxen to a breaking plow and plowed a dozen furrows around the camp's perimeter.

A firefighting crew battles a fire in Big Falls, Waupaca County, 1910.
WHI IMAGE ID 25650

Then, while filling water barrels on a barn roof, one of the men said he saw a cloud of smoke in the distance. As John climbed up on the roof to have a look for himself, the wind quickly picked up, bringing the fire with it. A broken stump some hundred feet from the sleeping shanty began to burn. The men threw water on it, but the fire spread to the logging camp buildings. It was only then that John realized the danger they were in.

He and his fellow workers raced toward a wall of green timber some five hundred yards away. The fire chased them. The other two men knelt to pray. John stood leaning on a tree, sure he was about to die. And then it began to rain. All three men survived.[3]

Of all the disastrous forest fires in Wisconsin, the fire of October 1871 was the worst. That spring and summer had been extremely dry; the last reported rain, just a trace, had come on September 5. In early fall, fires had flared up near Oconto, Pensaukee, and Little and Big Suamico, and for at least a month, locals had fought the fires and saved many structures. But the fire burned on in nearby timber. On the afternoon of Sunday, October 8, a slight breeze had blown, picked up, and then stopped, leaving a dead calm. "It was like the silence of the grave," remembered Reverend Kurt R. F. Geyer.[4]

As residents of Peshtigo turned in that night, some saw a dull red glow near the horizon. Later they heard a low rumbling, then a roar. They jumped from their beds and rushed into the streets. Seeing the conflagration approaching the town, citizens gathered to fight the fire. Soon, flames leapt above the treetops and approached the village. Burning coals began dropping everywhere, as some survivors recalled, "like snowflakes in winter." Buildings near the woods caught fire. People rushed toward the river, believing the flames would stop at its banks. Many jumped into the water and drowned. Others died on the way, succumbing to the deadly smoke and flames. A few found safety in a low marshy area east of the river.

In only a matter of minutes, the entire village was in flames. With tornado-like intensity, the wind tore the roofs off buildings and knocked fleeing residents to the ground. Survivors reported that even the air

(continued)

seemed to be on fire. The next morning, the village of Peshtigo was no more.[5]

The fire that came to be called the Great Peshtigo Fire devastated other parts of northern Wisconsin as well. The village of Williamsville, near Brussels, was destroyed entirely, and sixty people perished. It was never rebuilt.[6]

Occurring the same day as the great Chicago fire of 1871, the Peshtigo fire killed between one thousand and fifteen hundred people. The conflagration virtually destroyed the timber in large portions of Oconto, Brown, Door, Shawano, Manitowoc, and Kewaunee Counties. With high winds fanning the flames, the fire burned an area ten miles wide and forty miles long.[7]

Notes

1. Wisconsin Historical Society, "Forest Fires in Wisconsin," no date, www.wisconsin history.org/Records/Article/CS1699.
2. F. Curtiss-Wedge, "The Lumber Industry," in *History of Wood County, Wisconsin*, ed. George O. Jones and Norman S. McVean (Minneapolis, MN: H. C. Cooper Jr., 1923), 11.
3. John L. Bracklin, "A Forest Fire in Northern Wisconsin," *Wisconsin Magazine of History* 1, no. 1 (September 1917): 17–24.
4. Rev. Kurt R. F. Geyer, "History of the Peshtigo Fire, October 8, 1871," *Peshtigo Times*, October 6, 1921.
5. Geyer, "History of the Peshtigo Fire."
6. Justin Skiba, "The Fire That Took Williamsonville," *Door County Pulse*, September 2, 2016.
7. Mark Wyman, *The Wisconsin Frontier* (Bloomington: Indiana University Press, 1998), 275.

Piling the logs at the riverbank was the most dangerous job of any in the woods. The men lifted the logs into the air using a block and tackle, and a worker called a top-decker steered each log into place. If the log swung too far or too fast, it could hit the top-decker and injure or kill him.

The *Shawano County Journal* in the winter of 1879–1880 reported, "The principal items from the woods this week have been in the shape of crippled persons coming in." The newspaper chronicled the past week's toll along the Wolf River and its tributaries: "One man killed when the chain broke on the load of logs he was driving; a Menomonie [sic] Indian logger badly injured when a falling limb hit him on the head; a man bruised when he fell off a load of logs going downhill, another bruised when he was pinned between two logs."[2]

Workdays for the logging camp crew were long. For some, especially the teamsters and log skidders, work stretched well into the evening. A teamster who was late getting out to the woods one morning offered this as the reason for his tardiness: "Well, you see, boss, I didn't get to camp from the last haul last night in time to get out this morning."[3]

Finally, when it was too dark to see, the lumberjacks returned to camp. They removed their boots and hung their wet clothing on a rack near the hot stove to dry. A long sink with three to ten wash pans, depending on the size of the crew, could be found at one end of the bunkhouse. By the time the men were washed up, supper was ready.[4]

FEEDING THE CREW

Although the foreman was the camp boss, the camp cook was king. The cook was comparable to a mess sergeant in an army camp: without good food in ample amounts, neither an army nor a logging camp could function.

Logging camp workers eat their fill after a long day of work. WHI IMAGE ID 5777

Frank E. Cummings, whose mother had worked in an Eau Claire–area camp as a cook, later worked as an assistant cook. By that time, most of the camp cooks were men. In a 1916 article, he described his work as a cookee: "The cook does the baking and gives general superintendence to the work. The 'cookees' prepare the vegetables, washes the dishes, sets the table, waits on table and scrubs the floors. It surprises some to learn that floors are scrubbed in a lumbering camp cook shanty, but a visit to a camp having a good cook would convince them that a cook shanty is usually a pretty clean place."[5]

Cummings described some of his cookee duties:

The task of waiting on the tables is comparatively simple. Tea or coffee and cold water are set on the tables at regular intervals, with a full assortment of all articles of food. It is the duty of the "cookees" to see that the food and drink is replenished as necessary. The men do the rest.

Hot water and soap with plenty of clear hot water for rinsing, puts the dishes in shape. The process of drying the silverware . . . after being washed and rinsed, while still hot, they are put in a clean grain sack and with a "cookee" at each end they are well shaken and emptied on to the table, perfectly dry and ready to use.

Lumberjacks on a dinner break in Glen Flora, Rusk County. WHI IMAGE ID 1960

The vegetables are kept in a "root house" [sometimes called a root cellar], which is sometimes a separate building, built of logs, partly underground and thickly covered with dirt. Double doors are used to keep out the frost and a pipe put in the roof for ventilation. Instead of a separate building very frequently the root house is built as a lean-to against the side of the cook shanty and a door cut through for access to same.[6]

Dell Chase worked as a cookee at age fifteen in a lumber camp near Kennan in Price County. At that camp, the cookee was known as a bull cook and had duties beyond the mess hall. As Chase recalled, "I started as a bull cook, that's the guy that gets wood and water for the cook, takes care of the bunk house such as getting wood, water, and sweeps and scrubs the floor. . . . The bull cook had the barns to look after, keep them clean, keep the teamsters' lanterns full of oil, clean the globes, and haul dinners out in the woods. There is no such thing as a noon hour in the woods. The men sit on poles around the fire to eat their dinner."[7]

Iva Trotier of the Rhinelander area worked as camp cook. In 1974, she wrote this recollection of her days in a lumber camp in the town of Enterprise in Oneida County:

It was October 1910, and my husband hired out for the winter with the Wenzel Brothers, Gus and Bill, for a logging job. . . . At the time he said they needed a cook and helper. I dreaded being alone all winter with our small son, so I talked it over with my husband's sister, Mary, six months older than I, not married, and we applied for the job. Mary was the oldest girl from a family of nine, and I was from a family of eight, so we did know something about cooking and work. The men went to get the camp ready ten days ahead, but notified us to get ready and be sure we had everything [we needed], as we wouldn't get out until late spring. . . . After seeming to be a long drive, lo and behold, we came out into a clearing on top of a little knoll, and below us on a level spot was our home to be for the winter. I will never forget it.

There below us was a long log building under one roof, a cook shanty, office and men's shanty. There was also a horse barn, a root cellar and meat house, tool shed and two little outhouses. . . . Running so peacefully nearby was a big creek and a lovely spring for drinking water. We unloaded and had four days to get organized before the crew came in. . . . There were tables and benches. Many of the provisions were packed in old-fashioned orange crates with the dividers in, so they were nailed to the log walls and served as cabinets. Mary slept on a folding cot, which when not in use was shoved under our bed. Our bedroom had two log walls, the end and one side. . . . The door was curtained with two gunny sacks sewed together. There was just enough room for our bunk, the baby's crib, a small chest, and two orange crates nailed to the wall. The first night we worked late filling shelves and finding where things were. We found the office also was the storage building. In it were sacks of sugar, flour, beans, peas, rice, macaroni, coffee, raisins, dried apples, apricots and the like. There were also tobacco, cigarettes, matches, wool socks, and mitts for the men to buy when they ran short. Also in the cook shanty was a barrel of sauerkraut and half a barrel of dill pickles, a large assortment of unhemmed dishtowels made of flour sacks and plenty of dishrags.

We made out our menus for a week and set to work. The dishes were all of tin—pie plates and large coffee cups, also dish-up bowls and platters—so there was no dish breakage. As soon as the dishes were washed after a meal, the table was set, ready for the next meal. The center dishes were never taken off, but were covered with a clean cloth after the meal. These were salt and pepper, mustard, catsup, sugar, and vinegar. . . . We baked ten loaves of bread every other day, besides making light cake, dark cake, raised doughnuts, fried cakes, cookies, bread pudding and pies. Thank heaven my little son was a good baby. We made a makeshift playpen out of a large box, put a blanket in the bottom, and put in his toys, and there he played unless he was hungry or needed other attention. He spent his first birthday in camp.[8]

Early camps had no stoves and relied on a fireplace for cooking and baking. "The baking was done in tin Dutch ovens, the rest of the cooking in camp kettles," noted lumberjack Thomas McBean. "The cooking was plain and consisted of bread, salt pork, beans, blackstrap molasses, potatoes, (when you could get them), coffee and tea. . . . If there was a hunter in camp, then [we had] some venison for a change.[9]

LOGGING CAMP FARMS

As Northwoods logging camps grew in size and number, supplying food to the hungry lumberjacks and feed for the oxen and horses became a constant challenge. To meet the demand, several logging companies operated their own farms. As early as the 1850s, Daniel Shaw's lumber company managed a nine-hundred-acre farm near the mouth of the Flambeau River. The Shaw farm produced cabbages, onions, rutabagas, potatoes, green vegetables, wheat, hay, cattle, and hogs. Knapp, Stout, and Company operated six farms on some seven thousand acres by 1874 and ground sixty thousand bushels of wheat annually at its own gristmill.[1] The Connor Lumber and Land Company's Camp Five, near Laona, Wisconsin, began operating as the lumber company's farm in 1914; the farm raised draft horses, animals for meat, and produce to supply both the company's camps and the company town of Laona.[2]

Notes
1. Joseph R. Conlin, "Old Boy, Did You Get Enough Pie?" *Journal of Forest History* 23, no. 4 (1979): 164–85; Mark Wyman, *The Wisconsin Frontier* (Bloomington: Indiana University Press, 1998), 263.
2. Lumberjack Steam Train, "Our History," no date, www.lumberjacksteamtrain.com /about_us.iml?ID=2.

Salt pork was common fare because the pork, salted in brine, would keep in warm weather as well as in cold. Baked beans were also part of many meals. Historian Malcolm Rosholt described how baked beans were made: "baked in a big earthen jar . . . [which] was banked with coals [in the evening] . . . and flavored with blackstrap molasses."[10]

McBean recalled the winter that his logging camp in the Chippewa Valley ran out of pork in midwinter. They did have a big supply of codfish. As he explained, "The river was frozen up, and all communication with the outer world was cut off until spring, so the codfish had to take the place in the cuisine of the dainty salt pork, but after a few jokes of the jacks about fish bones sticking out of their backs so that they could not get their shirts off in the spring, all were happy, and codfish, bones, and all went [all were eaten]."[11]

MODEL MENUS

Good food and plenty of it was essential for a group of hungry lumber-jacks. One account of life in the camps explained the need this way: "A logger would work in the mud, rain . . . risk life and limb a dozen times a day, do without company showers, sleep in drafty bunkhouses, all with a minimum grumbling, but start cutting back on the quality and quantity of cookhouse meals and he would quit immediately and spread bad words about that camp's food wherever he went."

In 1917, the US Food Administration suggested model logging camp menus to assure that the quality of logging camp food remained high. The instructions included six menus for breakfast, dinner, and supper, such as:

Breakfast

Oatmeal mush

Rye bread, cornbread and
    syrup, doughnuts

Cornmeal cookies, apple
    butter

Creamed potatoes

Coffee

Codfish cakes

Dinner

Rice and tomato soup

Roast beef and gravy,
    mashed potatoes

Bread and butter

Boiled onions, hulled corn

Apricot rolls, blackberry jam

Supper

Potato salad

Baked beans

Hulled corn with gravy

Nut bread and butter

Stewed prunes and molasses
    cookies

Note

Joseph R. Conlin, "Old Boy, Did You Get Enough Pie?" *Journal of Forest History* 23, no. 4 (1979): 171–175.

With few passable roads, it was a challenge to provide sufficient food for the camp workers and feed for the animals. Lumberjack William Alft provided this account of how the challenge was met for logging camps along the Wolf River in 1896:

> With the many camps scattered along the river from the Indian Reservation line as far north as Post and Pine lakes, there was need for an unusual supply of food and clothing for men; and hay and oats for the horses. Each camp had at least one tote team hauling supplies from Shawano to their respective camps, and in the fall, forty to fifty four-horse teams were busy on this road hauling supplies. It sometimes occurred that a wagon broke down or a horse was injured on the road, and a load of supplies was several days late. When this happened, the camp ran out of supplies, and I can remember when all we had to eat was boiled potatoes, syrup and pancakes. We used to go out of camp in the evening and listen for the tote wagon to come in, and what a welcome sound it was to hear the rattle of the wagon.[12]

New Hampshire–born Martin Page came to Wisconsin at age seventeen and soon found himself working on a keelboat that hauled supplies to logging camps in the Chippewa Valley. As Page recalled:

> The keel boats were about six feet wide, thirty to forty feet long and perhaps four and one-half to five feet deep. . . . The keel boats were rounded off on the bottom, with a keel plank running the full length of the boat. The front end of the bow was pointed, also the stern, but to a lesser degree. A steersman sat in the stern and helped to direct the course of the boat by means of a wooden arm secured to an upright post, into which the rudder blade was fastened. On both sides of the boat extending full length were planks called "running boards," about fifteen inches wide. . . . Eight men besides the steersman constituted the crew. The boats were propelled by poles, much like pike poles used by river men in the sorting of logs. . . . Four men worked on each side of the boat. . . . [They thrust] their poles on the river bottom and the knob or button against their shoulders, they walked quickly to the stern, drew up their poles and ran back to the bow, when the operation was repeated.[13]

Recreation, Religion, and Rest

The lumberjacks' life in a remote logging camp, with long days in the woods and even longer nights spent in smelly, crowded bunkhouses, could be tedious. The men had a few hours free after the evening meal and before bedtime during the week, and Sunday was generally a day free of work.

In the evening, by the light of a kerosene lantern, the men kept busy with "mending socks, darning mittens, sewing up rents in old clothes, whittling a goad stick [long stick with a pointed end for prodding oxen], making an ax helve [handle], dressing out an evener, blocking out an ox yoke, connecting pieces of broken chain with cold shuts, fixing harness, grinding axes, reading aloud from some paper or magazine, telling stories, or . . . singing."[14] Around them rose the aroma of the wet clothing they had shed after returning to camp, now spread on racks near the stove. As one account described the scene, "When the socks began to dry, you sure knowed you were in a logging camp. When you mix the smell of wet socks with the smell of baked beans and chewing tobacco, you have a smell that a lumberjack never forgot even if he lived as long as Methuselah."[15]

Socks dry above the heads of tired lumberjacks in Cable, Bayfield County, 1902.
WHI IMAGE ID 5055

BRINGING CHRISTIANITY TO THE CAMPS

In 1892, the Young Men's Christian Association, or YMCA, held a conference in Eau Claire to discuss the possibilities of bringing the work of the YMCA to the logging camps in northern Wisconsin. The organization had been successful in doing so in Canada and Michigan. Its goal was described as "prosecuting a moral Christian work among the men in their camps."

Charles Hamilton had been a student at the Moody Bible Institute in Chicago and was expected to do outreach work. The YMCA was an organization through which Moody Bible Institute students could fulfill this mission. The YMCA saw one of its goals to extend its programs with "the most specific and widely heralded mission to a particular group of workers was a long-sustained effort in behalf of timber crews on the part of the state [YMCA] committees of Wisconsin and Minnesota."[1]

Hamilton, an Englishman born in 1873, was a newcomer to Wisconsin's Northwoods. He knew little about logging camps, with their rough-and-tumble workers, many of whom were far better at cussing than reciting Bible verses. Hamilton was turned away at some camps, but generally he and his partner, Alfred Terry, were allowed to present their program, which consisted of singing and a short sermon. They saved time to speak individually with camp members who wished to talk with them. Hamilton drove a one-horse cutter (a light sleigh) with the letters YMCA printed on the side.[2]

For three months in the winter of 1892–1893, Hamilton and Terry visited 80 logging camps in northern Wisconsin, addressed 4,000 men, converted 56 to Christianity, and gave out 75 Bibles and testaments and 6,150 magazines, books, papers, and tracts. They traveled 920 miles with horse and cutter, 600 miles by rail, and 110 miles by foot.[3]

Notes

1. Robert Weidensall, *Beginning and Early Development of Wisconsin YMCAs*, State Work Series, vol. 5 (New York: YMCA Historical Library, 1913), 237–38.
2. Charles C. Hamilton, *The Northwoods Journal of Charles C. Hamilton: An Englishman in Wisconsin's Lumber Camps, 1892–93*, ed. Mary Hamilton Burns (Rudolph, WI: River City Memoirs, 1992), 15.
3. Hamilton, *The Northwoods Journal*, 15.

Some of the men played poker; some just rested on their bunks and smoked their pipes. Sometimes there was a little singing, some fiddle playing if one of the lumberjacks had that skill. But mostly that type of entertainment waited until Saturday night and Sunday.[16]

Then it was off to bed. "Generally the only argument at night was whether it was too hot or too cold. One sleeper would get up and open the skylight to cool the room, and someone else would get up and close it. Often the bull cook had to settle the argument, and he generally kept it too hot. Skylight ventilation was preferred because it lessened the

Fiddling and dancing in the bunkhouse, date unknown. WHI IMAGE ID 55608

odor of a hundred socks drying around the big stove in the middle of the bunkhouse."[17]

Sunday was a day of rest in the logging camps, except perhaps for shoeing horses and oxen and repairing equipment. An itinerant lay preacher might visit, usually just before mealtime, and those interested in hearing him speak would assemble in the dining hall. But Sundays were mainly devoted to washing clothes. The water was heated in a large iron kettle set over a fire. The washtub was usually a wooden barrel sawed in half. A washboard was the only washing "convenience" available to the men. Lice was a common problem in most camps; boiling clothes not only cleaned them but solved the louse problem as well. No baths were taken—it was rather common for lumberjacks to go an entire winter without a bath, and generally without ill effects. During the warmer months of the logging season, a wash bench and barrel of rainwater stood outside the bunkhouse where the workers could wash their hands and faces. Soap and towels were usually supplied. Most of the men also shaved on Sunday, and a crude homemade barber chair was typical in most lumber camps for hair cutting.[18]

Sunday morning—and shaving day—in a Chippewa Falls camp, 1900. WHI IMAGE ID 1963

Drinking was not allowed in the logging camps, "not for moral reasons," according to historian Rosholt, "but because some men never knew when to quit, and when drunk became violent or abusive. The men lived in close quarters, and violence of any kind could upset the peace in the bunkhouse."[19]

The men's recreation during those hours when they were not chopping or sawing wood was taken up with card playing, practical jokes (especially for the "greenhorns"), and preposterous stories of vicious creatures of the woods. One such story was that of the Hodag.

The Hodag story had been making the rounds of the logging camp bunkhouses in Wisconsin for several years before it was ever seen. Newcomers to a logging camp were often told of this fierce animal, which was the size of an alligator and roamed the Northwoods with a terrifying scream that raised the hair on the neck of the bravest new lumberjack. To make the tale more vivid, occasionally an old-timer lumberjack would sneak off into the woods on a cold winter night and yell the bloodthirsty call of the Hodag.

But the Hodag was only a story until 1893, when Eugene Simeon Shepard, a real estate speculator, one-time logging camp foreman, and timber cruiser in the Rhinelander area, claimed to have stumbled onto the vicious creature. He reported his sighting to the locals in Rhinelander, saying that he had met "face to face with a 185 pound, seven-foot-long lizard-like beast. Its head was disproportionately large for its body with two horns growing from its temples, large fangs, and green eyes. Covered with short black hair, the body appeared stout and muscular; its back was covered with spikes, which led to a powerful tail. The four legs were short and sturdy with three claws facing forward and one in the opposite direction . . . its nostrils spouted flame and smoke, and a horrible odor, which . . . [could be described] as a combination of buzzard meat and skunk perfume."[20]

The report of Shepard's sighting, with an accompanying sketch of the ferocious creature, appeared in the October 28, 1893, issue of the *New North*, Rhinelander's weekly newspaper. Shepard's tale, so elaborately told and detailed, caught the attention of several lumberjacks who were game to organize a local posse with the intent of capturing alive this menace of the pinery. Armed with rifles and sticks of dynamite, they began searching for the beast. Finding the ferocious creature, and now on to Shepard's elaborate hoax, the group lobbed dynamite at the beast. They brought the charred remains of the Hodag back to Rhinelander, stating they were not able to capture it alive.

Shepard sought to continue the hoax—and did so quite successfully. He claimed to have captured a live Hodag in the fall of 1896, which he exhibited at the Oneida County fair in a dimly lit tent. He showed the creature at several other county fairs and, some reports say, at the Wisconsin State Fair. After the fair tour, Shepard kept the Hodag in a shed at his home, where many more people had an opportunity to see it. Eventually, the elaborate hoax was uncovered. The body of the Hodag was a carved stump covered with an ox hide. Its horns and spike were from oxen and cattle. Hidden wires caused the "creature" to move, and the growl was that of Shepard's hidden son.

The hoax fooled hundreds if not thousands of people and brought considerable notoriety to the city of Rhinelander, which even today is known as the Hodag city. A larger-than-life representation of the menacing beast can be seen outside the Rhinelander Area Chamber of Commerce building.

Replica Hodag in Rhinelander. PHOTO © STEVE APPS

PAUL BUNYAN TALES

While the mythical Hodag is purely a Wisconsin creation, stories of Paul Bunyan are widely recognized across the United States, especially in the northern logging regions. A traveler can find Paul Bunyan restaurants, resorts, and other tourist attractions from Maine to Oregon, and especially in the upper Midwest. As author Michael Edmonds noted, more than three hundred books, plus numerous recordings and videos, feature Bunyan and his famous blue ox and their many, often preposterous, tales.[1]

Paul Bunyan stories were believed by many to have originated in eastern Canada and the eastern states where logging preceded that in Michigan, Wisconsin, and Minnesota. Tall tales from the woods came west with the lumberjacks—tales about days so cold that spoken words froze in the air and snow so deep it reached the tops of trees. But according to Edmonds, there were no Paul Bunyan stories in the East. He wrote, "The earliest trustworthy mention of the name Paul Bunyan dates from the winter of 1885–1886, when two detailed, independent descriptions came

from Tomahawk, Wisconsin."[2] The first verifiable mention of Paul Bunyan occurred when retired logger Bert Taplin recounted hearing Bunyon tales from a timber cruiser named Bill Mulhollen while visiting a logging camp near Tomahawk during the winter of

An artist's depiction of Paul Bunyan and Babe, his blue ox. WHI IMAGE ID 55609

1885 or 1886. A second source was Jim McKeaque, a logger in the same vicinity, who recalled in 1938 that he had heard the tales the same winter in Tomahawk.[3]

The oral versions of Bunyan tall tales likely go back to at least 1880. The first of them appeared in print in 1904. The outlandish tales were told again and again in the camps and often were embellished in each new telling. One told of Paul tying a rope to the end of his ax and cutting forty acres of pine with a single swing, "and thus he cleared the Dakotas of trees." The narrator would insist, "Go to the Dakotas. You won't find any pine." In another, Paul Bunyan's famed blue ox, Babe, could reverse the flow of the Mississippi River merely by taking a drink from it.[4]

Paul Bunyan contributed to a larger-than-life lumberjack mythology after 1925 when the oversized woodcutter became a symbol of something more than merely a worker in the woods. "Skillfully embellished tales about him by professional writers captivated the nation," Edmonds explained, and "millions of Americans eagerly embraced him as their nation emerged on a world stage, grappled with economic collapse, and faced up to a second world war."[5]

Here are a few examples of Paul Bunyan tales, slightly rewritten:

It seems the cook at the logging camp was late blowing the dinner horn. Bunyan burst into the cook-shack, grabbed the dinner horn, and pointed it out the window. With one long blast of the horn, the concussion uprooted eighty acres of pine and laid them flat.[6]

Paul Bunyan's double-barrel shotgun required a keg of railroad spikes to load each barrel plus four dishpans full of powder. He could shoot geese flying so high that they would spoil before hitting the ground.[7]

Paul Bunyan had his own cook, his cousin Big Joe. Big Joe made hotcakes on a griddle so large you could not see across it when the steam was thick. It was greased by boys who skated over it with hams on their feet.[8]

Notes

1. Michael Edmonds, *Out of the Northwoods: The Many Lives of Paul Bunyan* (Madison: Wisconsin Historical Society Press, 2009), 1.
2. Edmonds, *Out of the Northwoods*, 31.
3. Michael Edmonds, personal correspondence, June 4, 2018.
4. Robert F. Fries, *Empire in Pine: The Story of Lumbering in Wisconsin, 1830–1900* (Madison: Wisconsin Historical Society Press, 1951), 233.
5. Edmonds, *Out of the Northwoods*, 5.
6. Edmonds, 190–91.
7. Edmonds, 190–91.
8. Joseph R. Conlin, "Old Boy, Did You Get Enough Pie?" *Journal of Forest History* 23, no. 4 (1979): 175.

5

FROM FOREST TO SAWMILL

The last glaciation of the land that would become Wisconsin left hills and valleys, boulders and sandy plains, and an abundance of lakes and rivers. The majority of the state's rivers run in two directions: in northeastern Wisconsin they run toward Lake Winnebago, and in central and northwestern Wisconsin they run toward the Mississippi River. If one were to drop a feather in the Wolf River in northeastern Wisconsin, it theoretically could find its way to the Atlantic Ocean. Another feather dropped in the Wisconsin River could travel as far as the Gulf of Mexico.

These rivers were the prime transportation routes of the day. Native people used the waterways as transportation routes for thousands of years before the first Europeans arrived. The French missionaries and fur traders used the rivers as major transportation routes when they arrived in the state in the mid-seventeenth century. So did the early pioneer settlers in the state.

The 1787 Northwest Ordinance established a system for land ownership in the Northwest Territory, making it legal for people to use the rivers of the area for purposes of transportation. Article 4 of the ordinance states that "all navigable waters leading into the Mississippi and St. Lawrence, and the carrying places between the same, shall be common highways, and forever free . . . without tax, impost or duty therefore." Article 34 of the 1849 Wisconsin Statutes carried forward the same rules, stating that "all rivers and streams in this state, in all places where the same have been [surveyed] . . . are hereby declared navigable to such extent that no dam, bridge, or other obstruction may be made in or over the same, without permission of the legislature."[1]

Therefore, it was logical that before the railroads arrived in northern Wisconsin in the early 1900s, the primary way logging companies transported logs to the sawmills was by floating them down the rivers.

The Log Drive

Of all the activities associated with the logging era in Wisconsin, none exceeds the romanticism associated with the log drives. Longtime logger John Nelligan wrote, "In the old logging days of Wisconsin and Michigan, every spring saw the curtain roll up on a tremendous drama along the rivers of the timber country; a drama greater even than that in which the giant pines were felled and dissected; the epic drama of the drive."[2]

Economist Frederick Merk described a log drive this way: "The drive was the most picturesque as it certainly was the most dangerous of the season's operations. Down the ice-cold torrent thousands upon thousands of logs went surging and hurtling, sometimes halting at an obstruction as if in hesitation and piling up in rude masses, then rushing onward again with greater momentum."[3]

Once the snow melted and ice went out on the rivers of the north, it was time to move the enormous piles of logs that had been stacked along the great rivers. Driving logs meant steering floating pine logs down a raging river during the spring melt. As was true of so many jobs in the early days of logging, driving logs was extremely dangerous. With tools no more sophisticated than a long pike pole, a shorter jam pike, and calked

A log drive crew on the Chippewa River, 1905. WHI IMAGE ID 37826

(spiked) boots, the men rode the logs as they rushed downstream, steering them away from the riverbanks and trying to prevent logjams. Many of the rivers had "dead man's bends," where a log driver had lost his footing and drowned, later to be buried on the hill overlooking the river.[4]

With the spring breakup and ceasing of timber cutting, most of the lumberjacks left the woods for their homes. But a few sturdy, adventure-some men stayed on, changing their rubber boots for those with spikes on the heels and soles so they could dig into a pine log floating in a river. As Nelligan described them, they were the pick of the lumber camp, "lum-berjacks of unusual strength, agility, daring, and hardihood. . . . For days they had to go with but little sleep and snacks for food snatched whenever and wherever possible. They had to suffer frequent duckings and were almost continually soaked to their skins. . . . They worked in a treacherous element, and the slightest misstep or miscalculation might send them relentlessly to their deaths."[5]

Now that winter was over, log drivers traded their heavy woolen shirts and pants for lighter cotton overalls, cut off just above the boot tops. Cotton would dry much more quickly than heavy woolen clothing. They wore flannel shirts and hats of every style and description.

Much was expected of these men who risked their lives to steer the lumber companies' logs from the riverbanks to the sawmills. As one writer stated, every log driver "was expected to accept his share of punishment from the river; the chill, the rain, the wet feet, and the lack of decent sleep-ing quarters. The ones who stayed on the job and did not quit after the first time they fell in or had to wade into the cold water to 'sack' a stranded log, were the bravest of the brave, physically tough, mentally alert, and with ice in their veins."[6]

Historian Mark Wyman described the log drivers: "The men started before dawn, rousted from their sleep and given the first of their four or five meals of the day, usually at the floating wannigan, which trans-ported their packs as well as providing meals. Out on the river, their red flannel shirts now the proud uniform of the north country, climbing onto a log moving downstream, digging their boot calks into the bark, jabbing their pike poles, the men challenged the vagaries of the river and early spring weather to maneuver a mass of logs through waters boiling with runoff."[7]

A tough group of log drivers tackle a jam on the Flambeau River near Ladysmith.
WHI IMAGE ID 78984

The essential tools of the log driver were the pike pole and the jam pike. The pike pole was about sixteen feet long, the jam pike about five feet. Both had a sharp point. When riding on the logs, the log driver would drive the jam pike into one log while standing on another; in this way he could relatively safely move down the river with its load of floating logs. The log driver used the long pike pole to move the floating logs into position as well as to reach those caught on shore or by some other obstruction in the river.

The cant hook, about five feet long with a hardwood handle and a hook on one end, was widely used in the woods, but not by the log drivers. In 1857, a Maine blacksmith, Joseph Peavey, created the Peavey by combining the cant hook and the jam pike. Log drivers found it extremely useful, as it could be used as a lever, as a jam pike, or as a gripping tool.[8]

Often, more than a hundred men were involved in a log drive. Driving individual logs down a river usually required three crews: "A rear crew who saw to it that all logs were put afloat, and none were left behind . . . a jam crew seven or eight miles below the rear crew, and another jam crew further down," according to William Alft's history of logging on the Wolf River. He continued,

In a studio portrait taken in Black River Falls, a young logger holds a peavey.
WHI IMAGE ID 46149

It was the duty of the jam crews to see that the river did not jam full of logs, and to keep an open channel for the logs to float down. The rear crew had two large boats called bateaus [*sic*], each boat about thirty-five feet long, and four to five feet wide coming to a peak on both ends. The boats were used to take men back and forth across the river and take men to "centers," that is logs that had hung up on rocks in the river. The boats could only be handled by expert boatmen, usually large, strong men with much experience in that line of work, as the lives of the men depended on them, as crossings had to be made many times over fast rapids and swirling waters.[9]

In addition to the bateau following in the rear of the drive with men looking for stray logs, a second wooden raft, usually called a wannigan (also spelled wanigan, wanegan, wanagan, wannegan, and used with slight differences in meaning depending on the region), followed the drive. The wannigan housed the cook and cook's helper, food supply and cast-iron cooking stove, the personal effects of the log drivers, plus tents and bedrolls. The wannigan also served as the temporary office for the chief river pilot.

Workers in bateaux on the Chippewa River at Jim Falls, 1909. WHI IMAGE ID 6317

A wannigan called the *Dancing Annie*, operated by the Chippewa Lumber and Supply Company, 1900. WHI IMAGE ID 119881

During a drive, for ten hours or so each day, the river drivers keep the logs straight and moving by pushing and prodding with their pike poles all the while trying to maintain their balance and avoid falling into the swirling, log-filled water. The entire operation was supervised by the chief river pilot.

At day's end, when the logs came to rest against the night boom, a temporary storage area along the river's edge, the men went ashore, set up their tents, and spread out their bedrolls. They lined up for the evening meal, which might consist of salt pork, potatoes, biscuits, coffee, and perhaps a piece of raisin pie. After supper, the men might spend their time greasing their boots with tallow and filing the calks on their boots. Then it was time for bed, and soon another day on the water.[10]

Log driving was different on each river, depending on the river's depth, width, number of waterfalls, and frequency of obstructions, such as boulders and low-hanging branches. For instance, the logging crews working the Wolf River region in northeast Wisconsin used the Wolf to transport their logs to the sawmills in Shawano, New London, Neenah, Menasha, and Oshkosh. The Wolf, while picturesque as it flowed some 225 miles from its source in Langlade County to Lake Poygan and on to Lake Winnebago, was relatively narrow. Crews working on the Wolf had to cut trees that had fallen into the river. In addition, sections of the river were strewn with huge boulders, some as large as eight feet in diameter and thrust above the water level from one to six feet. To clear the way for logs, crews blasted these boulders from the water, making a clear path. It was extremely hazardous work.[11]

LOG-DRIVING ASSOCIATIONS

In the early years of the logging era, there was little coordination among the companies driving logs down the rivers and streams each spring. Starting in the late 1800s, several log-driving associations were organized. One of the first was the Wisconsin River Exchange and Log Driving Association, formed in 1875. Some of the log-driving associations were cooperative endeavors organized by the sawmill owners; others were independent, for-profit organizations.

In 1870, sawmill owner Philetus Sawyer of Oshkosh, Henry Sherry of Neenah, and several other mill owners organized the Wolf River Improvement Company to make the Wolf River navigable for logs.[12] As part of the river improvement effort, workers constructed a series of driving dams along the river. Using the dams, the river level could be controlled and the various river rapids and falls could be flooded, allowing the logs to move freely downstream.

Workers constructed the dams by building square boxes in the river and filling them with small rocks and gravel. These boxes, called cribs, provided the foundation for a dam. On the upstream side of the dam, from the top of the dam to the riverbed, workers placed a row of planks tightly fixed together to hold the water back and create a pond behind the dam. Many of these dams also included gates that could be raised and lowered with winches of various kinds. Raising the gates allowed the logs to pass through the dam.[13]

Many tragedies occurred at the dams. Lumberman William Alft recalled one incident:

> About the year 1878, soon after driving was started on the Wolf River,
> a sad accident occurred in the spring of that year. Six men were left
> at the Gardner Dam to raise the gates very early in the morning. But

the water from Post Lake dam arrived earlier than expected, and the crew of six men awoke at 12:00 o'clock midnight and found that the water had arrived and was flowing over the dam. The foreman, a man by the name of Kennedy, took his men out on the dam and started to raise the gates. As soon as the gates started to rise, the terrific pressure of the water forced the dam, and with a terrific roar the dam went out carrying with it the six men.

A crew maneuvers logs through rapids below a dam, 1890. WHI IMAGE ID 77721

Two men who were sleeping in a tent nearby heard the crash and jumped out of their bunks. Above the roar of the rushing water they heard the cries of the men who were being swept to their death. Running to the river bank to give what assistance was possible, they at once came upon a man who was washed on the logs nearby, and succeeded in dragging him to shore. . . . The other five were drowned or dashed to death on the rocks and amid the wreckage of the dam.[14]

RIVER PILOTS

In the early days, logging companies tended to employ their own men on the log drives each spring. Some of the drives were successful, but many were not, as many logs were lost and too many men were injured or killed. River pilot companies formed to offer their services to lumber companies.

Archie Young, a pilot and logging camp foreman for the Arpin Lumber Company, navigates the Wisconsin River, 1886. WHI IMAGE ID 7577

Most of the river pilots were lumberjacks who worked in the woods in the winter and then hired out to a river pilot company in the spring. A river pilot's salary for one month could equal the salary he received for three months in a logging camp. But the lumberjacks hired on by the river pilot companies had to meet stringent requirements. As one writer noted, these men needed "the agility of a cat, an incredible sense of balance, the ability to make correct, split-second decisions or you could be injured or even killed, the endurance to work ten hours in partial or totally wet clothing, the stamina to be just as sharp in the aforementioned qualifications as you were at the beginning hours . . . on two meals a day."[15]

MARKING AND MEASURING LOGS

At the height of the spring log drives, several logging companies often sent their logs down the river at the same time. To solve the problem of sorting out which logs belonged to whom, each company's swamper stamped the company's unique brand on the end of every log using an axlike device. The marks were recorded in the district office of the lumber inspector, and anyone who altered a lumber mark or used another company's mark was subject to a fine.[16]

These stamps, used to designate ownership of logs, are part of the collection at the Paul Bunyan Logging Camp Museum in Eau Claire. WHI IMAGE ID 53220

The logging companies were paid by the number of board feet of lumber they had cut during the long winter months in the woods. Scaling meant doing an approximate measurement of the board feet in a log (a board foot is 144 cubic inches, or 12 inches by 12 inches by 1 inch thick). A white pine, depending on its size, could yield more than 2,000 board feet; some of the largest pines yielded enough lumber to build a small house. Many disputes emerged when the scalers' estimates of board feet differed from the actual number of board feet sawed at the mill. To respond to the enormous number of disputes between logging companies and mills, the Wisconsin legislature passed a law in 1861 to create a surveyor general position with responsibility for providing uniform log scaling for much of the state. The legislation created four logging districts: the Wisconsin River

Scalers measure logs on the Chippewa River. WHI IMAGE ID 25748

and its tributaries, the Black River and its tributaries, the Chippewa River and its tributaries, and the St. Croix River and its tributaries. A district surveyor general was appointed to maintain an office in each district and provide sufficient deputy scalers. These men, at the request of the lumber companies in the district, measured the company's logs before they were transported to the mills. The deputy scalers were paid, as stipulated in the law, by the logging company at the rate of four cents per thousand feet of logs measured.[17] By 1878, the state legislature had established twelve main logging districts in the state; by 1898, there were seventeen.[18]

LOGJAMS

Running individual logs down a river often resulted in logjams and lost logs. In a logjam, some obstacle prevented the logs from moving freely downstream, but the logs kept coming, resulting in a massive pile of tangled and twisted logs. An 1869 logjam on the Chippewa River was estimated to contain up to 130 million board feet of logs and extended up the river for two miles.[19]

In 1879, a logjam occurred on the Jump River, a tributary of the Chippewa, that extended nearly sixteen miles upstream. During a log drive in the 1880s on the Wolf River, logs jammed on the rocks at the foot of a waterfall, holding back the logs that followed. Ultimately, a tangled stack of logs sixty feet high resulted, requiring a crew two weeks to clear. In 1880, a jam occurred at Wausau that backed up for several miles. Also in that year, a logjam at the head of the Lily Dam flowage on the Wolf River involved an estimated 30 million board feet of lumber and took a crew twenty-two days to break it up.

In 1884, an enormous logjam occurred on the Wisconsin River north of Wausau at Grandfather Falls, where the river dropped some one hundred feet in less than two miles. That spring the log drive had begun at Eagle River, and an ever-increasing number of logs joined the river from various tributaries that drained into the Wisconsin. About a million board feet of pine had been cut that winter, and two-thirds of the logs had safely moved over the falls with the early spring high water. But when the water dropped enough to expose the rocks at Grandfather Falls, about 32 million board feet of lumber got caught. For more than a month, men worked to break up the jam, but they could not do it. Jim Crane, who lived in Oshkosh and had broken up many logjams on the Wolf River, was summoned. For two weeks, Crane worked, using dynamite to break up the jam and send the logs on their way to Wausau, Stevens Point, and Grand Rapids (now Wisconsin Rapids).[20]

It was not uncommon to use explosives to clear a jam. Sara Witter Connor explained, "The dynamite was planted for the strategic log to burst the jam by a 'pickman.' Often he died at the scene as the logjam burst open and the power of the logs moving did not allow an escape."[21]

A notable logjam occurred at Angel Rock on the St. Croix River in 1886. It took several weeks to clear the jam even with the help of two Mississippi River steamboats. Sightseers came from St. Paul by horse and buggy to watch some two hundred men and a hundred horses working at the site.[22]

A massive log jam on the St. Croix River. WHI IMAGE ID 62818

Historian Malcolm Rosholt wrote that the most extensive log-driving dam in the history of Wisconsin was built on the Chippewa River near present-day Holcombe. The dam had twenty-eight gates. It was below this dam, on July 7, 1905, that eleven log drivers met their death when they were sucked into the fast-moving current. A logjam had developed at the dam, and seventy-five log drivers from Chippewa Falls rode seventy-five minutes on the train with the hope of breaking it up. When they arrived, the jam had reached a height of 250 feet. Sixteen men in a bateau, "some carrying whiskey from the night before, and everyone in a holiday mood," attacked the jam. Five of the men leapt onto the jam, but the bateau capsized with the remaining men aboard and "threw the men against the rocks and logs like toys in a bathtub."[23]

Rafting Logs and Lumber

A practical alternative to moving logs singly was to tie them together in large log rafts.

In 1843, a group of Mormons were among the first to demonstrate rafting logs, using the method on a drive from the Black River to Nauvoo, Illinois. Also in that year, a boom broke on the St. Croix River, allowing a large number of logs to escape. The logging company gathered the loose logs together at Stillwater, Minnesota, and formed them "into four rafts of a million board feet each."[24]

Starting in the 1840s, logging companies using the Mississippi River realized rafting logs was the better way. Steamboats were used to move the log rafts on the St. Croix River as early as 1848 and on Lake Winnebago in the 1850s; by the 1860s, steamboats were moving log rafts on the Mississippi River.[25] And on the upper Mississippi, large-scale rafting of logs began in 1887 and peaked in the 1890s.[26]

On the Black River, most of the logs were formed into rafts and floated to La Crosse at its mouth. The logs not sawed there were floated down the Mississippi River to markets in Iowa, Illinois, and Missouri.[27]

The best approach for driving logs varied considerably from one river to another. The Wisconsin River, with its many turns, rapids, and waterfalls, made log driving extremely difficult, so sawmills were built as near as possible to where the logs were cut.

Rafting logs on the Chippewa. WHI IMAGE ID 68937

The challenge then was to move the sawn lumber downriver, and rafting lumber became common practice. The smallest section of a lumber raft, called a crib, was sixteen feet square. Each crib contained twelve to twenty tiers of one-inch-thick boards. Six cribs placed end to end comprised a rapids piece, so named because it was designed to move through rapids. According to geographer Mary Dopp, two to eight men were required to handle a rapids piece, using thirty-six-foot oars and moving a number of rapids pieces at one time:

> A fleet consisted of fifteen or more rapid pieces, [and was] managed by one pilot and his assistants. . . . Below Grand Rapids [Wisconsin Rapids], two "rapids pieces" coupled side-by-side formed a "Wisconsin raft" with which the river men ran the Dells. Below the Dells several rafts were united, but not until the Mississippi was reached was the

whole fleet united into one great raft one thousand to fifteen hundred feet long and two hundred to three hundred feet wide. Upon this cabins and cookhouses were erected and the hands were able to get regular meals and sleep. The first large raft reported to have been taken down the Wisconsin went from Portage to St. Louis in 1839.[28]

Ceylon Childs Lincoln, a lumber raftsman, described going over the dam at Stevens Point on his first time lumber rafting down the Wisconsin River.

My first experience in rafting was in 1868 when I went down with Homer Chase of Stevens Point as pilot. . . . The ice went out on the river April 17, and the next day we started with five men at each oar, to run the Stevens Point dam, near where the lumber had lain throughout the winter.

We ran down the center of the river, until within twenty rods of the dam. There the current drew off to the right and came in between two piers, about thirty feet apart; between these piers was the slide, constructed of long logs (called "fingers") fastened with chains to the dam; on either side of the slide, the water dropped about fifteen feet. Below the dam, the river boiled and rolled into whitecaps. If one was fortunate enough to make the slide properly, he could make his landing in the right place; otherwise there was great danger of saddle bagging one of the piers and breaking it to pieces. Sometimes the raft turned a complete somersault, and the men who did not leap for the pier were drowned. Even when going down the slide, our rafts generally sank until we were standing waist-deep in the water, bumping along on the rocks. . . .

We seldom had a chance to go to the raft on which the cook shanty was placed, for our meals. Our food was brought alongside of us by a small skiff that accompanied the fleet. The fare was very good, considering the way in which it is served.

We never floated down at night, but each raft tied up, with a half-inch cable to the bank. When our day's work was finished, we would run the raft close to the bank; the talisman would jump ashore and make the end of the rope fast with a hitch, while the bowsman secured it to the raft itself. Our rope, being old, often broke; then we would ground [the raft] by shoving a plank down between the pieces until it scraped the bottom and checked the momentum. . . . Our fleet was loaded with newly sawed shingles . . . there was quite a traffic in [stealing] shingles during the night. There would come a dip of oars, and a skiff would draw alongside the raft, and want to trade whiskey for shingles. It was surprising to see what a lot of shingles it took to purchase a quart of poor whiskey. . . .

When our fleet arrived at the mouth of the [Mississippi] River there was great rejoicing, as the hard work was mostly over. The nine Wisconsin rafts were coupled into one large Mississippi raft, with a cook shanty in the middle, and long table where men could be seated for meals. Our Mississippi River Raft consisted of three Wisconsin rafts abreast and three deep, making a raft 144 feet wide and 380 long.[29]

The Dells at Kilbourn (now Wisconsin Dells), where the Wisconsin River narrows between high rocks on either side, proved one of the most difficult places to navigate lumber rafts. Many raftsmen drowned attempting to navigate this treacherous place in the river. Miriam Bennett, daughter of famed Wisconsin Dells photographer H. H. Bennett, searched early copies of the Kilbourn weekly newspaper for lumber rafting stories and the harrowing adventures the raftsmen faced going through the Dells of the Wisconsin. She wrote, "In 1856 'Dutch' Jake Weaver drowned in the Dells when his oar caught in a whirl. The next spring, with the Wisconsin running wild, several rafts broke up in the Dells. Timing the river in flood, for half a mile at the Narrows, the current was said to run at fifteen mph. A raftsman was drowned and Leroy Gates, working as a river pilot, had four of his eight rafts damaged at the dam."[30]

According to Bennett, river pilot Leroy Gates, apparently quite taken with his own reputation, once advertised in the newspaper that he "stood at the head of the pilots for coolness, intrepidity and courage." Bennett also mentioned a story told about Gates who set to pilot "a raft through the Narrows [in the Dells] in full formal attire, but his finery was not impressive when the raft broke up, and he had to dash for the safety of shore with his coat tails flying and his silk hat . . . bobbing in the river."[31]

H. H. BENNETT

Early photographer H. H. Bennett sought to capture the exciting activity of lumber rafts passing through the dangerous stretch of the Wisconsin River now known as the Wisconsin Dells. In 1886, with a camera, a homemade shutter, and Cramer dry plates, Bennett went aboard the Arpin Lumber Company's fleet of rafts at Kilbourn and traveled as far as Boscobel on an eight-day trip. In a letter Bennett wrote to D. J. Arpin, the photographer said, "We had a glorious time and made lots of pictures, how good they will be I cannot say as I have not developed the plates. Most of all I have done an illustrative of the raftsmen's life, leaving the scenery along the river for another season."[1]

In her book *H. H. Bennett Photographer: His American Landscape*, Sara Rath wrote about Bennett's life and his work chronicling Wisconsin's logging era, when the raftsmen and their rafts constructed of sawed pine lumber passed through the dangerous narrows of Wisconsin Dells. Visitors to today's Wisconsin Dells can tour the H. H. Bennett

H. H. Bennett titled this 1886 photograph "Running the Kilbourn Dam, On Board the Raft." WHI IMAGE ID 4270

Studio and History Center in downtown Wisconsin Dells to learn about Bennett's life and see his famous photographs.

Note

1. Miriam Bennett, *Camera Man of the Dells* (unpublished manuscript, no date), 36–43. Available at McMillan Memorial Library, Wisconsin Rapids, WI.

Log Booms and Booming Companies

Logs owned by as many as 150 different logging companies might mix together as they tumbled down the river each spring on their way to the sawmills. To make it easier to sort the logs so the logging companies could be paid the proper amount for their winter's work, log drivers used booms, or spots on the river where the logs could be temporarily stored and sorted. Booms were constructed either in a natural area, such as a quiet bay or slough, or by chaining logs together end to end to create a fence that was then anchored to the shore and to the riverbed. Log drivers used pike poles to sort the logs by brand and move them into the corresponding booms.

Two men on a 1,150-foot-long swing boom on the Chippewa River above Alma.
WHI IMAGE ID 25790

With thousands of logs floating down Wisconsin Rivers by the 1850s, logging companies asked the Wisconsin legislature to issue charters authorizing individuals and companies to construct booms, build dams, and make other river improvements that would make it easier to move

THE BEEF SLOUGH WAR

From the early 1870s into the early 1890s, the most extensive boom works in Wisconsin were located at a place called Beef Slough north of Alma along the east bank of the Mississippi River and extending northeast along the Chippewa River for several miles. It was naturally formed and was a perfect place for lumber companies with sawmills along the Mississippi River to store their logs. The Beef Slough supposedly got its name when a government boat loaded with beef cattle on its way to Fort Snelling, Minnesota, got stuck on a sandbar. The crew unloaded the cattle, and the place became known as Beef Slough.[1]

The Chippewa River lumbermen, organized as the Chippewa River Improvement Company, resented "invaders," as some of the locals called the lumbermen who operated sawmills along the Mississippi River in Iowa, Illinois, and Missouri. The locals first tried legal means, but ultimately, in an action that become known as the Beef Slough War, they sent three hundred men to build a dam blocking the entrance to the Beef Slough. The county sheriff and a posse arrived, removed the dam, and arrested the ringleader and several other log drivers.[2] A historical marker erected near Alma in 1976 declared that the most important outcome of the Beef Slough War "was the arrival on the scene of Frederick Weyerhaeuser, whose Mississippi Logging company brought skilled capital into the picture and changed the logging operations on the Chippewa from locally-operated activities into a major interstate industry."

Notes
1. Ralph W. Hidy, Frank Ernest Hill, and Allan Nevins, *Timber and Men: The Weyerhaeuser Story* (New York: Macmillan, 1963), 45.
2. Mark Wyman, *The Wisconsin Frontier* (Bloomington: Indiana University Press, 1998), 268; Malcolm Rosholt, *The Wisconsin Logging Book, 1839–1939* (Rosholt, WI: Rosholt House, 1980), 168.

logs down the rivers. The legislature passed more than one hundred boom acts and more than two hundred dam acts between 1850 and 1873.[32] In addition, the Wisconsin legislature was responsible for granting charters for each boom company until 1878. The boom companies made money by charging logging companies a specific rate for each log entering their boom.[33]

By 1870, every logging district in the state had a log boom and log improvement company. In the Wisconsin River District, the Little Bull Falls Company was organized in 1852. The first boom company on the Black River began operations in 1854, and the Chippewa River Booming Company was organized in 1855. In 1856, the Wisconsin River Boom Company was formed, with huge booms at Wausau. The Wolf River Boom Company was organized in 1857.

6

LOGGING AND
LUMBER LEADERS

Operating a logging company was a risky and challenging business in the 1800s, and it demanded a unique set of skills. Purchasing timberlands and buying logs required a keen eye for quality and the ability to negotiate a price that allowed the company to earn a profit. Understanding the complicated lumber market, with its constant ups and downs, demanded sharp financial skills. Moving logs, lumber, and supplies long distances across complicated terrain and treacherous waterways was an immense undertaking. Finding a skilled crew was challenging, and because of the dangerous nature of the work, company owners had to deal with constant injuries, and even deaths, among staff.

The logging company owners attracted to the vast pine forests of Michigan, Wisconsin, and Minnesota came from diverse backgrounds. More than half of them had been born and raised on farms, and few had formal education beyond eighth grade. More than four-fifths of the leading lumbermen were born in the northeastern states or in eastern Canadian provinces. Frederick Weyerhaeuser and Benjamin and Sigmund Heinemann, all born in Germany, were notable exceptions.[1]

During the years of rapid expansion of the logging industry, several hundred logging companies worked Wisconsin's Northwoods. The most successful were led by owners and managers with that unique combination of business acumen, sufficient finances, and good management skills. Notable leaders in logging and lumber throughout the late 1800s included Isaac Stephenson, John P. Arpin and sons, Nelson Ludington, Cadwallader C. Washburn, Daniel Wells, Philetus Sawyer, Thadeus Pound, Daniel Shaw, J. G. Thorpe, John H. Knapp, James Huff Stout, the Connor brothers (Robert, John, and James), and Frederick Weyerhaeuser.[2] By the 1890s, a quarter of all Wisconsin workers were employed in logging and lumber businesses. They created immense wealth for the company owners, who in turn invested in other Wisconsin industries and contributed to the growth of their communities.

WEYERHAEUSER

Frederick Weyerhaeuser was born on November 21, 1834, in Germany. After leaving Germany in 1852, he worked in Pennsylvania and then, in 1856, moved to Rock Island, Illinois, where he worked for a railroad and eventually owned and operated a sawmill. By 1860, he partnered with his brother-in-law, Frederick C. A. Denkmann, and they employed several men.[3]

During the 1860s, Weyerhaeuser and Denkmann continued milling operations in Rock Island, Illinois, purchasing logs from rafts at Rock Island or from the Black River at Onalaska, Wisconsin. The partners relied on the open market for their logs until the late 1860s. In 1872, Weyerhaeuser purchased his first timberland.[4]

The partners were among the first sawmill operators along the Mississippi River to buy land in northern Wisconsin and thus harvest their own logs. According to historian Mark Wyman, Weyerhaeuser's "invasion into the Chip-

Frederick Weyerhaeuser. WHI IMAGE ID 3777

pewa Valley did not sit well with the logging companies already operating in the region. Wisconsin logs were not to be 'stolen' by 'aliens,' to be milled at 'foreign points.'"[5] Indeed, many squabbles arose between the local lumbermen and Weyerhauser; one resulted in the so-called Beef Slough War (see page 76).

By 1879, Weyerhaeuser, an astute businessman, suggested a cooperative agreement among what once had been warring parties. In 1880, the Mississippi firms and local Chippewa Valley logging companies met in Chicago and formed the Chippewa River Logging Company, also known as the Chippewa Pool. The Chippewa Valley lumber companies had 35 percent ownership and the Mississippi sawmills 65 percent in the Chippewa Pool. The agreement allowed the individual logging companies to continue to operate even though Weyerhaeuser was the dominant force in the organization. This new organization quelled the bitter competition, and Weyerhaeuser's fortunes continued to rise. In 1880, Weyerhaeuser acquired the Brunet sawmill in Chippewa Falls, at the time believed to be the largest mill in the world.[6]

By 1890, with the exception of Knapp, Stout, and Company's holdings, Weyerhaeuser ruled the Chippewa Valley timber resources. In that year, Weyerhaeuser was president or a leading officer in ten companies associated with Northwoods lumber.[7]

In 1900, with timber stands in the Chippewa Valley nearly depleted, Weyerhaeuser began moving his timber interests west. The American Immigration Company was organized in 1907 with responsibility for disposing of Weyerhaeuser's vast land holding in the Chippewa Valley. Two years later, the once highly successful Mississippi River Logging Company dissolved. Weyerhaeuser died in Pasadena in 1914.[8]

KNAPP, STOUT, AND COMPANY

It was in spring 1846 that William Wilson was traveling by steamboat on the Mississippi River and learned of a productive stand of white pine in the Chippewa River Valley. Leaving the steamboat, he walked to the site of present-day Menomonie, along the Red Cedar River. There he discovered a small sawmill operated by partners Black and Green (first names unknown). Green was eager to sell and leave the Northwoods behind. With a guide and a canoe, Wilson paddled some fifty miles to inspect the timber. Satisfied that this indeed was rich pineland, he traveled back to his Fort Madison, Iowa, home to seek funds to buy Green's interest in the

Staff members in the offices of Knapp, Stout, and Company, 1898. WHI IMAGE ID 103300

little sawmill and convinced twenty-one-year-old John H. Knapp to invest. They bought Green's share of the sawmill for two thousand dollars and operated it for a time as Black and Knapp. After Black's death in 1846, Knapp and Wilson paid off the executors and took over full ownership and operation of the mill.[9]

They hired Andrew Tainter as a foreman in 1850. Henry L. Stout of Dubuque, Iowa, bought a quarter interest in the operation in 1853, and the firm became known as Knapp, Stout, and Company. With Stout's capital, the firm rapidly expanded. By 1870, the company controlled the Red Cedar River Valley. Its lumberjacks cut hundreds of acres of pine, and when the pine was gone, farmers bought the land.

In March 1878, the company incorporated with capital stock of two million dollars, and Knapp, Stout, and Company soon operated sawmills at Menomonie, Rice Lake, Prairie Farm, Downsville, and Chetek, plus others in Dubuque and St. Louis. In 1878, the company was believed to be the largest manufacturer of lumber in the United States, employing some twenty-five hundred men. As historian Robert Fries pointed out, "Knapp, Stout, and Company represented what was perhaps the maximum growth of which a single concern was capable. It came as near being a monopolistic unit as the economics of the lumber industry permitted."[10]

With its surplus capital, Knapp, Stout, and Company invested heavily in land purchases. In addition to logging, the company developed urban communities such as Rice Lake in Barron County. By 1882, the company's capital had increased to four million dollars. Knapp retired from the firm in 1886 and died in 1888; Wilson died in 1892.

The city of Menomonie was headquarters for the firm's vast activities, which included sawmills, stables, stores, machine shops, blacksmith shops, a grain warehouse, and a grist mill. The company owned its own steamboats, which guided lumber rafts down the rivers and brought supplies for the various company-owned operations on the return trip. By 1900, when almost all of the Chippewa Valley pinery had been depleted, Knapp, Stout, and Company sold about 275,000 acres of its once pine-covered land and shifted its lumbering interests to the forests of Arkansas and Missouri.

Knapp, Stout, and Company essentially built the city of Menomonie. Several of the company's owners—Wilson, Tainter, Knapp, and Stout—built homes in the city. While the owners made millions of dollars from their lumbering operations in the region, they also gave back to the com-

The Mabel Tainter Memorial Building in Menomonie, built 1889–1890 with money donated by Andrew Tainter of Knapp, Stout, and Company. WHI IMAGE ID 39254

munity, helping to establish the first schools in Dunn and Barron Counties, contributing to local churches, and in the case of Tainter, endowing a civic center as a memorial to his daughter, Mabel. James Huff Stout, Henry Stout's son, contributed some of his wealth to establish what is now known as the University of Wisconsin–Stout. James Huff Stout also served as a state senator from 1895 to 1910.

CONNOR LUMBER AND LAND COMPANY/
CONNOR FOREST INDUSTRIES

In 1871, three Connor brothers, Robert, John, and James, originally from Scotland, left Stratford, Ontario, Canada, and arrived in Wood County, Wisconsin. The brothers found themselves in a forest of "the most magnificent oaks, maple, birch, and pines in the world," Robert's son William Duncan "W. D." Connor later recalled. The brothers took up farming and set out to develop the village of Auburndale, soon applying for a post office.[11]

In 1876, the Connor brothers purchased a sawmill, and two years later they added a planing mill and a shingle, lath, and stave mill. They built a company-owned blacksmith shop, school, hotel, and bank and opened a store. All the while, the Connors were purchasing hundreds of acres of forestland in Wood and Portage Counties. Thanks to the nearby Soo Line of the Western Central Railroad, they could transport their lumber by rail.

Unlike most loggers of the day, who were interested only in harvesting pine, the Connors saw a future in hardwoods. But the recession of 1882–1885 dimmed the previously bright picture for the Connor brothers. John and James Connor moved to Iowa and Kansas. Robert continued operating his business, now with his son, W. D., who bought timberland as his business strategy. When Robert was elected to the Wisconsin legislature in 1888, W. D. began managing the company and in 1890 incorporated it.

W. D. Connor became president of the company in 1892 and focused on expanding the R. Connor Company operations. He purchased Chicago and North Western Railroad lands near the Rice Lake Flowage and founded the village of Stratford in Marathon County in 1891. There he built company houses, a general store, and a post office. In 1894, he established the first band sawmill at Stratford; in that year he owned seven sawmills and contracted with three additional ones, producing 40 to 50 million board feet of lumber a year. The company constructed the Marathon County Railway to connect with the Chicago and North Western Railroad, allowing the company to ship more hardwoods from northern Wisconsin.

When many other industries suffered during the Depression beginning in 1892, the R. Connor Company purchased thousands of acres of timberland, often at reduced prices. The company also acquired land in northern Ashland, Iron, and Forest Counties in the late 1800s and early 1900s.

By 1890, the farm developed by the Connor brothers and now owned by W. D. Connor included 1,200 acres—immense, considering that 160 acres was a more typical size farm at that time. There Connor raised horses for his logging camps as well as beef, pork, and produce for the lumber camps and stores. The farm also raised many acres of hay and oats for the hundreds of horses the company owned.

In 1898, W. D. Connor and Mr. Langer, the R. Connor Company timber cruiser, arrived in Forest County, where they later purchased

William D. Connor, 1914. WHI IMAGE ID 61114

land. Connor founded Laona, a company town, and two years later, he established the Connor Lumber and Land Company as a separate company from the R. Connor Company with a different directorate. W. D. Connor eventually purchased about one hundred thousand acres in the area. The company bought a used sawmill in Eau Claire and moved it to Laona, where it added a planing mill; in 1902, it organized the Laona and Northern Railroad and built a dam on the river to create a pond for logs to be processed in the mill.

In 1898, the Chicago and Northwestern Railroad extended its services from Wabeno to the new town of Laona, where it built a depot, warehouse, and turntable. With expanded employment opportunities at the Connor sawmill, Laona grew to a population of seven hundred. The company built a hotel, houses, and a company store, then added a lath mill and a large flooring factory. The Connors built a hospital in 1902 and a school in 1903 and formed an electric power company and a telephone company.

In the early 1920s, the third generation of Connors, W. D.'s sons William Jr. and Richard M., became active in the Connor enterprises. A third son, Gordon R., was studying business administration and finance at the University of Wisconsin and was expected to join his brothers in the firm. Their father had decided it was time to expand the company's operations once more, and he began purchasing blocks of choice hardwoods in Upper Michigan. The company flourished.

By the mid-1920s, the Connors had remodeled their flooring plant and built a new sawmill. The company's management was also heavily involved in the community. Connor management served on the town board, library board, and school board. William Connor Jr. served as town chairman from 1924 to 1930. He was president of the Laona Bank and the Laona and Northern Railroad. For its workers, the company provided steady, long-term employment. Laona was one of the last true company towns, and it was the Connor Lumber and Land Company that made most of the decisions in the community, from the rent workers paid for their homes to the prices they paid at the company store.

With William Connor Jr. as general manager for the various operations of the company in Laona and Richard Connor serving as wood manager, the company became more diversified. It soon offered sawdust and wood shavings for sale and began manufacturing furniture for children. The company was also a pioneer in placing its timberland under the Wisconsin Forest Crop Act, which required selective cutting so that forests could regenerate naturally. Richard Connor and R. B. Goodman assisted with the creation of the Forest Crop Act passed by the Wisconsin legislature in 1926.

William Connor Sr.'s youngest son, Gordon R. Connor, graduated from the University of Wisconsin and then joined the family business in 1929. He became the manager of the R. Connor Company's Stratford operations, which moved to Michigan in 1934. By 1935, in the depths of the Great Depression, the R. Connor Company was taken over by the Connor Lumber and Land Company.

When William Connor Jr. entered the US Navy in 1942, Richard Connor took over as company manager. After William Connor Sr. died in 1944, Richard became president and Gordon R. Connor vice president of the company. In 1965, Richard became chairman of the board, and Gordon became company president.

In 1968, the company changed its name to Connor Forest Industries. In 1972, the company owned about 250,000 acres of timber in Michigan and 100,000 acres in Wisconsin, employing more than a thousand people and operating five sawmills in Michigan and Wisconsin. It established an assembly plant in Morristown, Tennessee, to service its national brand of cabinets. The company also made educational toys, puzzles, and blocks at Connor Toys in Wausau in the late 1970s.

In 1982, Connor Forest Industries was sold to a Swiss firm. Family members continued their interest in the forest industry. Gordon P. Connor bought the Wisconsin land holdings in northeastern Wisconsin as well as the Laona mill. His son, Peter, established W. D. Flooring, a manufacturer of premium residential and commercial hardwood floors. The Richard M. Connor Jr. family also has interests in several logging business subsidiaries and land holdings. Other members of the Connor family serve on the nonprofit board of directors of the Camp Five logging museum, established in Laona in 1969 by Gordon R. Connor and Mary Roddis Connor.

Gordon R. Connor was a member of the National Hardwood Association and was its president from 1968 to 1972. He was inducted into the Wisconsin Forestry Hall of Fame posthumously in 1986. In 2008, W. D. Connor was inducted into the Maple Flooring Manufacturers Association Hall of Fame. His induction statement in part read, "Not only is he the father, grandfather, and great-grandfather of continuing lumbermen and flooring manufactures, but he can also be considered the great-grandfather of modern milling and forestry practices. . . . [He] first established and incorporated the great tradition of sustainable forestry. [He] combined that sustainable philosophy with a tireless pursuit of modern processing technologies to continually save and preserve our most valuable renewable resource—our forest."[12]

WISCONSIN LUMBER IN THE WAR EFFORT

Wisconsin provided an assortment of wood products to support the US effort in World War II, including planes, gliders, boats, truck bodies, and shipping containers. As Sara Witter Connor wrote in *Wisconsin's Flying Trees in World War II*, "Over one hundred uses of wood would contribute to the Allies' victory. Many more were developed before the war was over."[1]

Among the orders received by the Connor Lumber and Land Company of Laona between January 28, 1942, and September 21, 1944, were the following:

July 8, 1942: "The Connor Lumber and Land Company received $887.50 from the Penokee Veneer Company in Mellen, Wisconsin, to provide lumber for crating."

August 6, 1942: "Richardson Brothers in Sheboygan Falls, Wisconsin, a furniture manufacturer, ordered $1,205.15 worth of lumber . . . for their conversion making rifle gunstocks for the army."

August 15, 1942: "Consolidated Power and Paper Company in Wisconsin Rapids, Wisconsin, ordered $1,723.05 of lumber. . . . Consolidated, with its subsidiary, Consoweld, was making glider floors and ammunition boxes of pressed phenol-resin paper product developed by the Forest Products Laboratory."[2]

During World War II, the Forest Products Laboratory in Madison was busy researching and developing a variety of new types of wood and paper products. For example, the laboratory developed a paper-based laminated plastic called Papreg. It was used for gun turrets, Army glider floors, glider seats, shields, and ammunition boxes for the B-24 Liberator bomber. Papreg was found to be superior to normal wood "in dimensional stability, hardness, electrical resistance, and other properties."[3]

The Forest Products Laboratory was instrumental in developing water-resistant plywood that could be molded into parts for military

(continued)

aircraft. The Beechcraft AT-10 trainer's fuselage, wings, and tail assembly were made of this plywood.[4] Waterproof plywood developed in the late 1930s by the Roddis Plywood corporation was used by Cessna, Beechcraft, Boeing, and other glider manufacturers; at one time, the Roddis Lumber & Veneer Company/Roddis Plywood Corporation was the only company in the United States producing waterproof plywood.

Notes

1. Sara Witter Connor, *Wisconsin's Flying Trees in World War II* (Charleston, SC: History Press, 2014), 15.
2. Connor, 15–16.
3. John W. Koning, *Forest Products Laboratory, 1910–2010: Celebrating a Century of Accomplishment* (Madison, WI: Forest Products Laboratory, 2010), 110–11.
4. Koning, 110.

Orrin H. Ingram

Born in Westfield, Massachusetts, on May 12, 1830, Orrin H. Ingram moved with his family to Saratoga, New York, where his father died in 1841. In 1847, at the age of seventeen, Ingram began working for the Harris and Bronson Lumber Company in New York. There he learned the logging business, working in the woods during the winter for twelve dollars a month and working at the sawmill during the summer for thirteen dollars a month. Some years later, Ingram managed the company's mill and helped it build another mill in Canada. He had many job offers in both Canada and the United States, eventually accepting one from the logging firm Gilmour and Company in Ottawa, Canada, believed to be one of the largest lumbering companies in the world at the time. Ingram was in charge of the firm's manufacturing business.[13]

By 1856, Ingram, having accumulated some wealth, decided to go into business for himself. With the gradual exhaustion of timber in the northeastern states, and recognizing the potential of the vast timberland in the Upper Midwest, Ingram moved to Wisconsin's Chippewa Valley. There, in 1857, he and his partners established the firm of Doyle, Ingram, and

FACING: In this 1880 view of Eau Claire, the Ingram, Kennedy, and Company mill can be seen at right, and another mill owned by Ingram is at left. WHI IMAGE ID 30693

Kennedy. They soon built lumber-yards in Wabasha, Minnesota, and Dubuque, Iowa; they built sawmills in Dubuque and Eau Claire. With Doyle's retirement in 1862, the firm became known as Ingram, Kennedy, and Company. In 1886, Ingram's firm built a steamboat, the *Silas Wright*, to move lumber rafts. It worked primarily between Reed's Landing in Minnesota and Eau Claire. The ship sank in 1892, when the lumber raft struck a buoy.[14] Ingram devised a system of lighters, or flat-bottomed barges, used to move lumber downstream

Orrin H. Ingram. WHI IMAGE ID 10674

where a river was too shallow for regular boats to navigate.

In 1880, Ingram sold his various lumber interests and, with capital of eight hundred thousand dollars, formed the Empire Lumber Company. He was active in several other lumber ventures, including organizing the

Rice Lake Lumber Company in 1883. Ingram bought timberland around Long Lake (Washburn County) from Knapp, Stout, and Company. To make transporting logs easier, Ingram built a dam at the south end of the lake, which raised the lake level by eight feet and thus connected three lakes that previously were separate. The area around Long Lake was logged by the Rice Lumber Company and Knapp, Stout, and Company from the late 1800s to about 1904.[15]

Ingram contributed to the Eau Claire area both in monetary contributions and personal involvement. He was active with the YMCA and donated money toward building a new YMCA building. He built a large office building in downtown Eau Claire called the Ingram Block (it has since been razed).

In describing Ingram in a history of Eau Claire, one writer noted, "Mr. Ingram, in his earlier day, could skillfully ride a log down a foaming current, knew how to get the lumber out of the woods, how to get it safely to the mill, and many days and nights were spemt out in the open among the woods and about the lumber camps. He ate beans and bacon along with his men, and when it was necessary he could put his shoulder side by side and hold up his share the equal of any lumberjack in his crew."[16]

BENJAMIN AND SIGMUND HEINEMANN

Born in Germany, Benjamin Heinemann immigrated to the United States and lived first in DePere in 1869 and then in Wausau in 1873. He operated a men's clothing store and then expanded his interests to banking, manufacturing, and the lumber business. He was the principal organizer of the Heinemann Lumber Company. His brother Sigmund, also born in Germany, immigrated to Appleton in 1871 and then moved to Merrill, where he operated a general store from 1880 to 1891. Sigmund became interested in the lumber business as well, and with a partner he organized the George E. Foster Lumber Company in Merrill. Their firm was one of the first to ship hardwood and hemlock lumber out of Merrill. In 1897, Benjamin joined his brother, and the business expanded with operations in Lincoln, Iron, and Marathon Counties. Sigmund was in charge of operations at Merrill, George E. Foster at Mellen, and Benjamin at Wausau.[17]

Walter Ben Heineman, Benjamin's son, was born in Wausau. He changed the spelling of the family name, dropping one of the *n*'s. Walter B. worked in his father's lumber business and in 1919 succeeded him as president of the B. Heinemann Lumber Company. Heineman was also active in politics, serving as chairman of the executive committee of the state Republican Party from 1913 to 1922 and vice treasurer of the Republican National Committee from 1928 to 1930. In addition to his state and national political activities,

Benjamin Heinemann, 1913. WHI IMAGE ID 62025

Heineman was a leader in Wausau community, at one time serving as a director of the American National Bank of Wausau.

COMPANY LEGACIES

Most lumber company owners were smart, effective businessmen, and many became very wealthy from their endeavors. For instance, in 1883, of the thirty La Crosse men worth more than $100,000, fifteen of them were lumbermen. In that same year, Eau Claire had fourteen lumbermen worth more than $100,000.[18] To put that wealth in perspective: the average full-time worker in Wisconsin in 1883 earned $363 annually.[19]

The work of logging and lumber workers was incredibly dangerous and difficult, and for the era, most of them made decent pay. Lumberjacks working in the pineries earned from three to four dollars a day, including room and board. Those driving logs down the river made more. But some companies did not treat their workers well. Economist Merk wrote that "labor conditions in the lumber camps continued throughout [the 1860s] to be most unsatisfactory. The food of the laborers was coarse and without variety, [and] the lodgings were unsanitary."[20]

The lumber barons, as these moguls of the industry were often called, accumulated great wealth through their enterprises. Some were unscrupulous in their lack of concern for their employees or for the impact their clear-cutting of the giant pines would have on the environment. Yet they contributed greatly to the economy and growth of the state. Until about 1900, Wisconsin's logging and lumber industries employed more workers than any other manufacturing industry in the state. In 1860, about two thousand men worked in the lumber industry; in 1890, that number was twenty thousand. And in the late 1800s, lumber paid more than any other industry, about $7 million annually. Nearly one-fourth of all wages paid to workers in 1889 came from the lumber industry.[21]

In addition, many of these leading business owners made impressive contributions to their local communities. The origins of scores of northern Wisconsin villages and cities can be traced directly back to the heyday of the logging era.

7

LIFE IN A SAWMILL TOWN

No single endeavor contributed more to the development of central and northern Wisconsin than the lumber industry. It was during the boom years that many villages and cities emerged. In many of them, including Marinette, Oconto, Park Falls, Peshtigo, Rhinelander, Tomahawk, Phillips, Mellen, Wausau, Stevens Point, Wisconsin Rapids, Black River Falls, Eau Claire, Chippewa Falls, Oshkosh, Green Bay, and La Crosse, the majority of the population depended on the local sawmills for employment.[1]

Like most other frontier towns, sawmill towns had sidewalks made of rough boards and muddy streets lined with simple clapboard homes and saloons. The primary social activities were dances and holiday celebrations. By the 1880s, a number of sawmill towns had baseball teams, and

Rice Lake traces its origins to the mid-1860s, when John Knapp purchased former Ojibwe lands near the Red Cedar River. A village grew up around the lumber company, seen here in 1872, and was platted in the 1870s and 1880s. WHI IMAGE ID 78293

logrolling contests drew crowds of observers. A logrolling competition consisted of a man perched on each end of a log, floating in a pond of water. The idea was for each man to attempt to dislodge the man on the other end by rapidly spinning the log and then stopping abruptly. By 1898, a national logrolling association had been formed that awarded a "world championship" award to the best logrollers. (The competition continues to this day as part of Hayward's annual Lumberjack World Championships.)[2]

The liveliest time of the year in the sawmill towns was spring, when the lumberjacks and river drivers returned from the woods and rivers with money in their pockets and a thirst for a rip-roaring good time. The saloon and the gambling establishments thrived during these celebration days that went on until the men ran out of money.[3] Brothels did a lively business as well. Author Michael Edmonds wrote about a brothel owner near Marinette: "Each spring he employed a woman, Mrs. Kassidy, to hire prostitutes in Chicago and Milwaukee in time for the arrival of the lumberjacks; some years he employed as many as sixty-five women."[4] Prostitutes weren't found only in Marinette; Green Bay, Superior, Ashland, and Hurley—almost every mill town had its red-light district.

A logrolling competition in Alma, date unknown. WHI IMAGE ID 25735

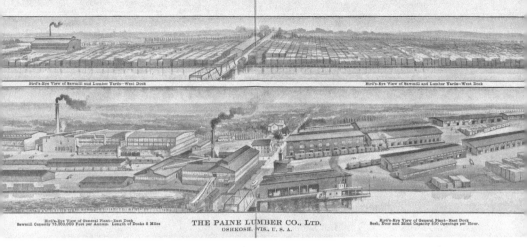

Bird's-Eye View of Sawmill and Lumber Yards—West Dock

Bird's-Eye View of Sawmill and Lumber Yards—West Dock

Bird's-Eye View of General Plant—East Dock
Sawmill Capacity 75,000,000 Feet per Annum. Length of Docks 2 Miles

THE PAINE LUMBER CO., LTD.
OSHKOSH, WIS., U. S. A.

Bird's-Eye View of General Plant—East Dock
Sash, Door and Blind Capacity 800 Openings per Hour.

A panoramic view of Oshkosh in 1902 shows the Paine Lumber Company's general plant, sawmill, and lumber yards. WHI IMAGE ID 80433

Of course, not all lumberjacks partied until their money ran out. Many were farmers who spent their winters trying to earn a little money in the Northwoods and in spring returned to their farms and families and the crops that needed planting.

By the late 1800s, a three-mile stretch along both sides of the Fox River in Oshkosh was lined with sawmills and related businesses, including shingle and planing mills and door, sash, and blind factories. As geographer Randall Rohe noted, "No other place in northern Wisconsin ever attained a more sudden celebrity as a manufacturing point than Oshkosh. From an obscure little village in 1852, with three or four sawmills, Oshkosh arose in only 10 years to the distinction of being one of the greatest lumber manufacturing centers in the Old Northwest."[5]

As many as forty places in northern Wisconsin were once major sawmill centers, and the population of the lumber towns in the north grew four times as fast as the population of the state as a whole during the years 1860 to 1870.[6] Some grew to be small cities, and some remained small; all were heavily influenced by the logging industry.

RHINELANDER

In 1857, nine years after Wisconsin became a state, what is now the thriving city of Rhinelander in northern Wisconsin was once "occupied only by trees and swamps through which the Wisconsin River splashed over Pelican Rapids seventy-one miles below its source in Lac Vieux Desert on the Michigan boundary."[7]

THE THREAT OF FIRE

Of all the challenges lumbermen faced, fire was the most horrific. A single spark in a sawmill could cause a holocaust, destroying the building and all of its contents and threatening the rest of the town. Starting in the 1850s, when sawmills were powered by steam engines fired by wood-burning boilers, the risk for fire was even higher.

In the early days of sawmill operations, it was common practice for the mills to dump sawdust into swamps or other low-lying areas. Vast areas around sawmills became prime candidates for raging fires, especially during dry years. By 1875, Oshkosh had gained the nickname "Sawdust City" thanks to a booming industry that included twenty-four sawmills, fifteen shingle mills, and seven sash and door companies. Wood byproducts littered the city, and piles of sawdust lined the riverbanks. Wooden sidewalks connected downtown businesses. Some buildings had been constructed on top of lumber waste.[1]

April 28 that year was sunny and dry. No rain had fallen for some time, and there was a brisk wind. Residents of sawmill towns were aware of the fire risks on such dry, windy days, and indeed, local sawmills were required to close on such days. But on this day, the Spalding and Peck mill had not abided by the requirement. Around one o'clock in the afternoon, sparks flew from the boiler's smokestack and ignited lumber piles at the

Fire at the McGillivray Sash and Door Company in Black River Falls, 1912.
WHI IMAGE ID 42624

Morgan Brothers mill nearby. One of the Morgan brothers attempted to extinguish the blaze, but he was unsuccessful and died as a result of his efforts. In short order, the Milwaukee and St. Paul depot and freight house were engulfed in flames. Soon, burning wood and embers flying on the fierce wind started fires a half mile away. The fire burned a mile-and-a-half stretch of businesses and homes.[2]

Historian Robert Fries reported that between 1885 and 1891, the value of sawmills in Wisconsin destroyed by fire exceeded $2 million, which was about half of the fire loss of all industries in the state.[3] Many mill owners quickly rebuilt, as the writer of an early history of Dunn County explained: "Sawmills and sawmill towns, flimsily constructed of inflammable pine, and consuming the airy fuel left by their saws, were periodically consumed by the flames. It was a rare sawmill that was not burned to the ground and rebuilt at least twice, while only one thing was more astonishing than the frequency with which sawmill towns were partially or wholly destroyed, and this was the speed with which they rose from their ashes."[4]

Notes
1. Karla Szekeres, "The Great Fire of 1875," Oshkosh Public Museum, 2015, www .oshkoshmuseum.org/oshkoshPublicMuseum/articlesOfInterest/the-great-fire-of -1875.
2. Szekeres, "The Great Fire."
3. Robert F. Fries, *Empire in Pine: The Story of Lumbering in Wisconsin, 1830–1900* (Madison: Wisconsin Historical Society Press, 1951), 105.
4. F. Curtiss-Wedge, "The Lumber Industry," in *History of Wood County, Wisconsin*, ed. George O. Jones and Norman S. McVean (Minneapolis, MN: H. C. Cooper Jr., 1923).

Not many miles to the south on the Wisconsin River, lumber companies built sawmills as early as the 1820s in what are now Mosinee, Wausau, and Stevens Point. Grandfather Bull Falls, sixteen miles north of Wausau on the Wisconsin River, presented a formidable barrier for log driving. At these falls, the river dropped 105 feet in less than a mile. Even though the land north of that point was rich in red and white pine, early loggers avoided working north of these treacherous falls. More than 150 sawmills had been established from Wisconsin Dells to Grandfather Bull Falls in twenty-five years beginning in the 1820s. But none were located north of the falls until, in 1855, a Mr. Helms of Stevens Point and his business partner, Joshua Fox,

The Thunder Lake Lumber Company in Rhinelander operated until 1934. WHI IMAGE ID 72459

hewed out a track wide enough for an ox cart and then, during the winter of 1857–1858, built a logging camp north of Grandfather Bull Falls. The following spring, the loggers successfully drove their logs to a sawmill at Mosinee, the first logs to pass what is now Rhinelander. When the Economic Panic of 1857 caused a downturn in the lumber industry, some of the lumberjacks in the Rhinelander-area camp decided to try new lines of work and started taverns, trading posts, and other businesses along the river. One of them was John Curran, who had been foreman of Helms and Fox's first logging crew. In 1858 or 1859, Curran built what he called the Half Way House on a former American Indian camping ground and thus became the first settler on the site that would become Rhinelander.

The Civil War began in 1861, and soon there was no manpower to work in the lumber camps—or anywhere else, for that matter. But with the war's end in 1865 and the completion of the US land surveys in 1866, the logging boom in the area began. It would continue for nearly three decades.

Logging speculators Anson Vaughn and Anderson Brown arrived at Curran's Half Way House in 1874 in search of timberland. They saw what is now Rhinelander as a potential site for a sawmill and boom operation on the Wisconsin River, and the Brown family bought fifteen hundred acres north of the Pelican River. The Browns platted the town of Rhinelander, named for F. W. Rhinelander of New York City, who was president of the Milwaukee, Lake Shore, and Western Railway. The Browns had grand plans for logging the surrounding area when they learned of the possibility that a railroad might come to the area. They convinced the Milwaukee,

Lake Shore, and Western Railroad to build a spur line to Rhinelander from Monico. The line was completed in 1882, and in the following year, the Browns built sawmills. In 1886, Frederick S. Robbins (known as FS) arrived in Rhinelander with partner S. H. Baird and formed Baird & Robbins, a logging and sawmill company. After Baird retired, Robbins partnered with the highly successful Brown brothers to form Brown & Robbins. By 1901, the company was known as the Robbins Lumber Company and had significantly expanded its extensive holdings to include two sawmills, planning mills, and a railroad; a 1902 article on the local lumber trade reported that the Robbins Lumber Company was "in operation day and night the year round."[8] Rhinelander was truly booming.

Tomahawk

Tomahawk's history traces back to 1886, when William H. Bradley, a lumberman with far-ranging business interests, arrived at the place where the Wisconsin, Tomahawk, and Somo Rivers come together. For fifteen years, Bradley had been buying timberland in the area, and he knew the region well. Bradley had building supplies hauled to the townsite he had selected by four-horse teams coming from Merrill. Getting supplies became easier when the Chicago, Milwaukee, and St. Paul Railroad trains began arriving during the winter of that year. Soon, Tomahawk boasted a hotel, box factory, bank, electric and telephone companies, opera house, newspaper, and department store. Bradley had a financial interest in each of these commercial concerns.[9]

With his two brothers and several other partners, Bradley organized the Tomahawk Land and Boom Company and began building a dam and a large sawmill on the Wisconsin River. But the forward-thinking Bradley was already looking ahead to a time when the vast timber would be no more, and he established a farm with a herd of purebred Jersey cows and a flock of turkeys. Alas, few farmers came to the area to follow Bradley's example.

With the sawmill up and running, Tomahawk grew rapidly. The town had a population of 2,300 by the early 1890s, with twelve hotels and thirty saloons. By that time, the Tomahawk mill was producing 75 million board feet of lumber and 25 million shingles.

The Bissell Lumber Company mill in Woodruff. Note the many cut trees behind the mill building. WHI IMAGE ID 55225

WOODRUFF

The area around Woodruff, in Oneida County, was rich in timber, but it was not on a significant waterway. Lacking the ability to transport supplies in or move logs out, logging companies avoided the area. Once the Lake Shore and Western Railroad arrived about 1888 (through consolidation, the railroad became a part of the Chicago and North Western system in 1893), logging quickly began. As one chronicle of Woodruff's history noted, "The advent of the railroad would open up the vast northern forests. The lumber 'barons' were 'licking their chops' with anticipation over the profits that could be made in this northern wilderness so they, with the help of their political friends, provided the momentum to get construction started. The development of the settlements in this area came as a direct result of the railroads." By 1910, large-scale logging was essentially over in the Woodruff area.[10]

SISTER BAY

The villages on the Door Peninsula were heavily influenced by logging activities. Located on a deep harbor on the bay side of the peninsula, Sister Bay became a favorite place for log-burning steam vessels to stop and refuel. As early as 1857, Norwegian settler John Thoreson built a dock there where he sold cordwood to ships. In 1868 and 1869, Hiram Coon and Thomas Diamond bought a little over three hundred acres that today comprise downtown Sister Bay. They built a dock and a sawmill where the Sister Bay Yacht Club is today and established a general store and a post office. After the death of Coon in 1875, Diamond continued operations until 1883, when he sold his interests to an employee, Andre Roeser, and Roeser's brother John. The Roesers continued logging in the area, including on Chambers Island. As the logging industry declined, the brothers added a lumber and hardware business that continues today as Lampert Lumber.[11]

Company Towns

By definition, a company town was one where a single lumber company owned the entire site, including most or even all of the buildings in the town. The company town's primary purpose, from the perspective of the lumber company, was to supply logs to the mill and convert those logs into lumber. A company town in Wisconsin's Northwoods generally included a sawmill, a planing mill, a machine shop, a horse barn, a lumberyard, and a hotel or rooming house for single workers. Most of the towns had limited "outside" business interests, but almost all had a company store where employees could buy essentials, often on credit extended by the company. The store might also include a post office and the lumber company's office. Sometimes one might find a shoe and boot shop, meat market, drug store, blacksmith shop, barbershop, or bank in these towns. Many company towns, especially after having been established for a few years, included a church and a school, and lumber company owners often brought teachers and doctors to serve the residents. Most companies did not allow a saloon or liquor store within their towns.

The lumber company was interested in attracting families to the town, with the married men working for the lumber company's various enterprises. But many single men also came to company towns to find work, necessitating the building of boarding houses and hotels. As might be expected, the largest and most architecturally interesting homes in the town were those occupied by the mill owner, the mill superintendent, and other high-level company supervisors.

Goodman, in Marinette County, was built and primarily owned by lumberman R. B. Goodman after fire swept through the area in 1907. To salvage nearby pine timber, Goodman founded the Goodman Lumber Company and almost immediately began buying additional timberland in northwestern Marinette County as well as in Forest and Florence Counties. Eventually, the Goodman Lumber Company owned about one hundred thousand acres of timberland. Along with the sawmill, the company built more than one hundred homes for workers, a hotel, a department store, a bank, and other buildings. It also added timber processing buildings, including drying kilns, a dimension mill, and a veneer mill.[12]

In 1908, the Soo Line Railroad built a spur to the emerging village. By September of that year, the company employed some seventy-five men, mostly carpenters, masons, and mechanics. As noted in a history of the town, "The company completed the boarding house in late summer 1908, at a reported cost of $10,000. It had eighty rooms and a dining hall capable of seating 200. It had steam heat, hot and cold running water, bathrooms, showers, and electric lights. . . . [W]ith work on the boarding house completed, workman started building the sawmill, with plans to build ten or twelve cottages in the next month."

McMillan, Salsich and Company built a mill in Jackson County in 1888 and named the village that sprang up there McKenna. After timber in the area was depleted, the mill operations left, and the townspeople eventually followed. WHI IMAGE ID 91795

The Goodman sawmill began operations in July 1909, and workers were soon filling the mill yard with enormous piles of lumber. The mill also powered an electric plant that provided electricity to the mill and the town.

The Goodman Lumber Company operated several logging camps to ensure the mill would have an ample supply of logs. The logs were hauled to the mills in two trips a day using the Goodmans' railroad, consisting of two locomotives and seventy-five flat cars.

When the Goodmans began their operations, like many other logging companies they practiced clear-cutting. By 1927, the company had cut about half of its virgin timber. That same year, with the enactment of the Forest Crop Law, which taxed land with standing timber at a much lower rate than land where the timber was cut, the Goodman Lumber Company began practicing what today is referred to as sustainable forestry, including the selective harvesting and replanting of trees. By instituting these sustainability measures, the company was ensuring a continuing supply of logs for its sawmill and other lumber processing activities.

The Goodmans sold the company in 1955 to the Calumet and Hecla Mining Company, with headquarters in Michigan. At the time of the sale, the Goodman Lumber Company still owned several homes and businesses in the village of Goodman, which had a population of about one thousand people. The new owners sold the remaining homes and businesses. Goodman was one of the last of the lumber company towns.

8

GROWTH, CHANGE, AND THE END OF THE ERA

Wisconsin's lumber industry continued to prosper into the 1870s, boosted by several innovations that increased efficiency and productivity. The introduction of the steam engine in the middle to late 1800s transformed the industry. Steam-powered towboats could move huge lumber rafts down rivers without depending on the river's current to move them. Steam-powered sawmills, no longer requiring water power to operate, could be located almost anywhere. Steam-powered railroads provided a safer, more dependable way of transporting logs than river log drives. And in the woods, huge steam-powered tractors hauled enormous loads of logs from where they were cut to a railhead for transport—any time of the year.

For a time, it seemed there was no end in sight to the logging boom. But as the end of the nineteenth century approached, even the loggers, who once believed the supply of pine logs was limitless, began to see an end of the softwood supply. Some of the logging firms moved on to establish operations in the northwestern United States or in the South where they developed pine plantations with a faster growing cycle. They left behind what came to be known as the cutover, a vast region of stumps and slashings.

STEAM POWER

In 1698, Thomas Savery, an English military engineer, invented a steam-powered machine to pump water out of coal mines. Savery's partner,

Thomas Newcomen, improved on Savery's primitive pump by inserting a moving piston inside a cylinder—a technique that is used to this day in steam engines. Savery's and Newcomen's inventions provided the foundation for the development of the steam engine, which was largely responsible for the Industrial Revolution in Europe during the eighteenth and nineteenth centuries.[1]

Steam-powered towboats first appeared on the St. Croix River in 1848, on Lake Winnebago during the 1850s, and on the Mississippi River in the late 1860s, cutting by half the time it took to move a lumber raft from a sawmill to market. At the peak of Wisconsin's lumber industry, more than one hundred steamboats plied the upper Mississippi River. The steam-powered towboat marked the end of the rafting crews that moved the lumber rafts along with the river's current. Some lumber companies owned their own steamboats, but most hired steamboats to move their rafts. The steam towboat always operated from the rear of a lumber raft. An anonymous lumberman complained in his journal in 1874, "The romance has gone out of lumbering to a great degree."[2]

By the 1850s, steam power began replacing waterpower in many sawmills, and therefore sawmills no longer had to be built on riverbanks. One

A steam-powered sawmill deep in the Wisconsin woods, 1910. WHI IMAGE ID 130920

of the first sawmills in Wisconsin to use steam power opened in Fond du Lac in 1846. At the time, Oshkosh and Fond du Lac sawmills were in fierce competition, and the owners at Fond du Lac hoped their new steam-powered sawmill would cement their superiority in the lumber and woodworking market. They succeeded in that effort for a few years, but Oshkosh once more became the dominant sawmill force on Lake Winnebago.[3]

Steam-powered sawmills were generally larger than water-powered mills, and they required more capital investment than those powered by water. Thus, they were concentrated in bigger cities such as Fond du Lac, Oshkosh, Eau Claire, and La Crosse. Thanks to the economies of scale, larger sawmills also encouraged the growth of related factories producing logging tools, sawmill machinery, furniture, trunks, and carriages.

Not all sawmill owners converted to steam power to run their operations. Where waterpower was abundant, as in Peshtigo, Oconto Falls, Chippewa Falls, St. Croix Falls, and Wausau, many owners continued using it to power their mills. The invention of the water turbine, patented in 1849, allowed many of the smaller mills to use waterpower; unlike a water wheel, a turbine operated with "dead water," meaning water backed up by a dam and then funneled to the turbine through a tube called a penstock.[4]

By the 1860s, a revolution in sawmill technology was fully under way. In Milwaukee, E. P. Allis and Company and Filer, Stowell, and Company began manufacturing machines to make sawmills more efficient. These included mechanical log turners, a variety of chains to drag logs to the saw deck, and steam-fed carriages that moved logs back and forth past the saw.

Some logging companies began using steam-powered log haulers to replace oxen and horses for toting logs from the woods to a rail line. The Phoenix Company in Eau Claire, a manufacturer of logging equipment, began producing what it called the Phoenix Log Hauler. It was a brute of a machine. Its steam engine produced one hundred horsepower; for comparison's sake, a team of horses could move one sleigh of logs at a time, while a log hauler could pull up to fifteen sleighs at a time.[5] Generally, the sleighs pulled by steam haulers were wider than the average sleigh, sometimes twelve or more feet wide. The amount they could pull depended on how level the ground was and how well the trail had been iced.[6]

A Phoenix log hauler pulls a load of logs through the snow at a Rice Lake logging camp, 1914. WHI IMAGE ID 5820

One lumber company manager described the log hauler this way:

The log hauler owned by our company, which is a Phoenix, was purchased in December 1907 at a cost of $6,000. We have used this steam horse for four winters, and during that time it has lost only one day, due to one of the parts breaking, which was quickly replaced by the manufacturers. Excepting this misfortune, the machine in question has missed but one trip in carrying out its regular schedule. [With the use of the log hauler] we have realized a big saving in the company and recommend it for the transportation of logs where the distance is five miles or greater, but it is not a good machine where the haul is less than five miles. . . . [U]nder load, its speed is from five to six miles per hour.[7]

A steam hauler required three men to operate it. Sitting at the front of the massive machine, the steersman worked a wheel similar to that of an automobile to keep the machine going in the right direction. The engineer, located in the cab behind the boiler, kept the machine running. The fireman made sure the boiler had sufficient fuel.

Railroads

Wisconsin's first railroad was the Milwaukee and Waukesha Railroad, chartered by Byron Kilbourn in 1847 to connect Milwaukee and Madison. Construction began in 1849. The state's first railroads were largely seen as connectors of Wisconsin's waterway transportation routes, intended to provide relatively quick and economical shipping between the Mississippi River and Lake Michigan. Thus, the first ones in the state were built leading west from the Lake Michigan port cities of Milwaukee, Racine, Kenosha, and Sheboygan.

Soon, however, the logging interests in the north realized that railroads provided an opportunity to expand their business by allowing access to a greater number of tree species. Not only did rail transportation replace dangerous log drives, it also allowed the loggers to cut timber a considerable distance from the waterways. The US government was exceedingly generous to Wisconsin's railroads, giving the state's railroads land grants of federal land exceeding 3.75 million acres in 1856 and 1864. As historian Richard Current explained, "Railroads were generally welcomed as the

Logging train in Star Lake (Vilas County), 1890. WHI IMAGE ID 126210

prime means of making available the natural resources and realizing the potential wealth of Wisconsin." In the minds of the federal government's lawmakers, the railroad supported the idea of Manifest Destiny, a term first used in 1845 to mean "that the United States was destined—by God, its advocates believed—to expand its dominion and spread democracy and capitalism across the entire North American continent."[8]

The Chicago and Northwestern Railroad made one of the first efforts to connect the pineries in northern Wisconsin to their markets in the south when it extended its line from Oshkosh to Green Bay in 1860 and then, in 1871, on to the Menominee River. Now the entire eastern Wisconsin pinery had an outlet to western markets by rail.[9]

By the early 1910s, lumbermen saw railroads as the answer to many of their problems. No longer would the loggers have to cut timber only during the winter months and stack the cut logs on a riverbank to wait for the spring breakup. Now logging could take place all year—itself a revolutionary idea. Additionally, with rail transport, logging companies could cut hardwoods such as maple and oak, which were increasingly in demand but did not lend themselves to river transportation. Logging companies quickly climbed on the railroad bandwagon.

In 1872, the Wisconsin Central Railroad advanced from the Fox River to Lake Superior, providing logging towns in central and northcentral Wisconsin with a new way of transporting lumber products.[10] In 1882, the Milwaukee, Lake Shore and Western Railroad extended beyond Antigo, and by 1883, it reached Pelican Rapids (now called Rhinelander).[11] As historian and author Sara Witter Connor has pointed out, "If you look at a map of Wisconsin, you see a straight line like a tree trunk and then 'branches.' The straight line is the railroad line to the sawmill, and the branches are the sleigh roads bringing the [logging sleighs] to the main railroad bed.[12]

Despite the encouragement and financial support of the logging companies and local and federal governments, the railroads came slowly to the north. As Connor noted, "The railroads did not get farther north until the 1890s. For example, W. D. Connor hiked from Gillette, where the railroad ended in 1898, to [the village] he would establish as Laona. The railroad had laid the route that it was going to take north, but it had not been completed."[13]

Unloading lumber at the McCormick Reaper Factory Works in Chicago, 1900.
WHI IMAGE ID 89191

But railroads eventually were built and others extended, and as they appeared throughout the north, the logging industry was transformed. Before the railroads arrived in the Northwoods, nearly all aspects of logging and lumber operations required that they occur near a stream or a river. Water transportation was the main way—in most instances, the only way—to move logs from woods to sawmill. Now, spur lines were built (many of them constructed by the logging companies) near where the logs were cut. When there were no more trees to cut in a region, the logging company pulled up the rails and moved them to the next location where cutting was to take place. With easy access to a railroad, a logging company could now ship its logs by rail.[14]

Railroads also changed the way sawmills operated. Before the arrival of a railroad, sawmills mostly produced undressed, rough lumber. But now, planing mills emerged that sawed logs and planed and dressed the lumber for market. Like the logging companies, the mills could ship their product any day of the year, not having to wait for the spring breakup to load their lumber on a raft and float it downriver to a distant planing mill.[15]

Environmental Concerns

As loggers moved across the north, they left behind the cutover, a bleak landscape of stumps and slashings. This vast area comprised the eighteen northernmost counties of the state and contained 11,767,090 acres, one-third of the state's land area. The region stretched from Oconto County in the east to Burnett County in the west.[16]

As early as 1854, Increase Lapham, a leading Wisconsin scientist of his day, wrote about the importance of forests, describing how forests influenced the state's climate, rainfall, and soil and warning of the dire consequences of allowing the clear-cutting of the north to continue unabated. Slowly, the Wisconsin legislature began to consider that something must be done. In 1867, the legislature passed a law creating a Forestry Commission. It appointed Lapham, J. G. Knapp, and Hans Crocker to the commission and instructed them "to ascertain and report in detail to the legislature at its next session certain facts and opinions relating to the injurious effects of clearing the land of forests upon the climate; the evil consequences to the present and future inhabitants; the duty of the state in regard to this matter."[17]

In the commission's report, Lapham minced no words about the likely outcomes if clear-cutting Wisconsin's vast pineland continued. He wrote, "Deprive a people of the comforts and conveniences derived directly or indirectly from forest products, and they soon revert to barbarism. It is

The barren landscape of the cutover. WHI IMAGE ID 105729

only where a due proportion between the cultivated land and the forests is maintained that man can attain his highest civilization."[18]

The report continued for 101 pages to support the commissioners' warnings. In his conclusion, Lapham wrote, "The commissioners having brought their work to a close, will state again that in their opinion, no other interest so much demands the immediate attention of the legislature of Wisconsin, as does that of increasing and preserving so much timber as shall be needed for future use by her people."[19]

The 1867 Forestry Commission's recommendations were prescient, but few people paid attention to its findings. The 1870s to the 1890s were peak years for logging in the pineland, and the logging interests wielded considerable political clout and monetary support for legislators approving logging efforts in the state. Logging continued to increase in the state every year until about 1900, except for the years of economic recession (1873 to 1878 and 1893 to 1897). In 1853, Wisconsin's Northwoods yielded an annual output of less than 200 million board feet of lumber; by 1892, over 4 billion board feet were cut—twenty times as much as in 1853.[20] During the boom years, it seemed that few could be convinced to care about logging's long-term impact on the environment.

The same was true when it came to the effects of sawmills. Sawmills created waste, including sawdust, edgings, and slab wood. To avoid being buried by their own waste, some sawmills used the sawdust to fill low land or pave streets, and vast areas around sawmills became prime candidates for raging fires, especially during dry years. The town of Kimball, in Iron County, with its streets and walkways paved with sawdust, saw a fire in 1904 that burned for weeks. In some rivers near where the mills stood, the waste material was mounded up to create islands, and in rivers near large mills, such as the Oconto, Menominee, and Peshtigo, harbors had to be periodically dredged of sawmill trash so river traffic could move.[21]

It was not until the late 1800s that Wisconsin legislators, some of whom were lumbermen themselves, decided something more definitive must be done about the growing problems related to the lumber industry, which included increased fire danger (both in the woods and in the sawmill towns), the impact of clear-cutting on the environment, and the question of what to do with lands once owned by loggers but now abandoned. At the state legislative session in 1897, lawmakers ordered a survey of Wisconsin's forest

Lumber waste produced by the Lake Shore Lumber Company of Oshkosh and dumped in a marshy area near Lake Tomahawk, 1900. WHI IMAGE ID 36589

conditions—although they did not appropriate any funds to conduct the survey. With the cooperation of the Wisconsin Geological and Natural History Survey, Filbert Roth, a forestry agent of the US Department of Agriculture (and later a professor of forestry at the University of Michigan), was asked to conduct the survey of the once vast pineland in central and northern Wisconsin. Roth's area of study was about 18.5 million acres, or about 53 percent of the state, and included twenty-seven counties north of a line from Green Bay in the east to the mouth of the St. Croix River in the west. The southernmost counties were Portage, Wood, and Jackson. Roth determined that of those 18.5 million acres, settlers owned 24 percent, most of it along the southern and southwestern edge of the district; the US government held title to about 5 percent; railroads owned a little over 5 percent; American Indian reservations accounted for about 2 percent; the state government owned about 2 percent; and the logging companies owned about 63 percent of these northern lands. Roth wrote, "Of [Wisconsin's] northern half, a land surface of over 18 million acres, only 7 percent is cultivated [in 1897], the rest forming one continuous body of forest and wasteland. . . . Of an original stand of 130 billion feet of pine, about 17 billion feet are left, besides about 12 billion feet of hemlock and 16 billion feet of hardwoods. . . . To remedy this matter and stop the great loss it will be necessary to adopt active measures both to protect and restock."[22]

A MODEL FOR SUSTAINABILITY

The Menominee Indians have called the land now known as Wisconsin home for more than five thousand years. At one time, the land they occupied stretched from the Great Lakes to the Mississippi River and comprised nearly 10 million acres. After a series of seven treaties beginning in the early 1800s, the Menominee land base was eroded to 235,000 acres, the size of their reservation today. The Menominee faced another setback in 1954, when the United States Congress passed the Menominee Termination Action, removing federal recognition and threatening, in the words of one critic of the action, "to deprive Menominee people of their cultural identity."[1] The former reservation became Wisconsin's seventy-second county in 1959. The tribe succeeded in winning back its federal recognition in 1973, regaining its legal status as a "Sovereign Indian Nation to which the federal government is obligated by treaties, agreements and statutes."[2] Today the Menominee live on a fraction of the land they once claimed as their tribal land; forestland covers roughly 95 percent of the reservation.[3]

Selective logging on the Menominee Reservation, 1938. WHI IMAGE ID 42573

In 1871, the tribe obtained permission from the federal government to harvest and sell timber from their lands, and by 1905 they were cutting 20 million board feet of timber annually.[4] But after a tornado blew down 40 million board feet that exceeded the Menominees' processing capacity, the tribe requested the assistance of US Senator Robert La Follette of Wisconsin. La Follette's legislation—the 1908 LaFollette Act—"contained language that assured a sustainable cut of timber, and authorized the establishment of a tribal mill [on the Menominee reservation]."[5] According to scholar and author Patty Loew, "La Follette's legislation was consistent with the tribe's own vision. It was designed to ensure that the Menominee would continue to selectively cut only mature trees . . . along with the trees affected by the blow-down."[6]

The Menominee had already long advocated for sustainable forest management practices, including selectively cutting mostly older trees and planting seedlings in a systematic way. The nation's sawmill, established in 1908 at Neopit, provides employment for many people living on the reservation today. Tribal foresters determine what to cut on the basis of sustainability practices without considering the needs of the sawmill.[7]

Researchers Donald M. Waller at the University of Wisconsin–Madison and Nicholas J. Reo at Dartmouth College have studied the Menominee and Ojibwe tribes' forestlands in Wisconsin. Their findings illustrate the long-term value of practicing sustainable forestry guidelines. Waller and Reo found that tribal-managed forests "are often more mature with higher tree volume, higher rates of tree regeneration, more plant diversity, and fewer invasive species than nearby nontribal forestlands. . . . Lessons from tribal forestlands could help improve the sustainable management of nontribal public forestlands."[8] The work of the Menominee Nation affirms the need for all Wisconsin citizens to look toward sustainable forestry to assure a future for our forested acres.

Notes

1. Menominee Nation, "Menominee Indian Tribe of Wisconsin: Brief History—About Us," no date, www.menominee-nsn.gov/CulturePages/BriefHistory.aspx.
2. Doris Karambu Onesmus, "Sustainable Management of Forest by Menominee Tribe from Past to Present," no date, www.uwsp.edu/forestry/StuJournals/Documents/NA/donesmus.pdf; Stephen J. Herzberg, "The Menominee Indians: From Treaty to Termination," *Wisconsin Magazine of History* 60, no. 4 (1977): 266–329.
3. Verna Fowler, "The People Who Live with the Seasons," in *Wisconsin Indian Literature: Anthology of Native Voices*, ed. Kathleen Tigerman (Madison: University of Wisconsin Press, 2006), 13.
4. Patty Loew, *Indian Nations of Wisconsin: Histories of Endurance and Renewal* (Madison: Wisconsin Historical Society Press, 2001): 28–29.
5. Loew, *Indian Nations*, 29.
6. Loew, *Indian Nations*, 29.
7. Ronald L. Trosper, "Indigenous Influence on Forest Management on the Menominee Indian Reservation," *Forest Ecology and Management* 249, no. 1 (2007): 134–39. https://doi.org/10.1016/j.foreco.2007.04.037.
8. Donald M. Waller and Nicholas J. Reo, "First Stewards: Ecological Outcomes of Forest and Wildlife Stewardship by Indigenous Peoples of Wisconsin, USA," *Ecology and Society* 23, no. 1 (2018), 45. https://doi.org/10.5751/ES-09865-230145.

Roth's words, like Increase Lapham's, fell on deaf ears. Logging continued at a rapid pace. Between 1899 and 1904, Wisconsin was the number
one producer of lumber in the country.[23]

Logging companies continued their march across the north, cutting
every pine in sight and leaving behind a mess of tangled limbs and treetops that were fuel for the massive fires that regularly roared through
the north. What remained was a desert of bare land studded with massive stumps standing four feet high and sometimes four feet and more in
diameter. Lapham and the forestry commission's predictions about the
cutover were coming true.

According to historian Mark Wyman, "Ecologically, no force since the
glaciers has rivaled northern logging in either its immediate or long-term
effects." Wyman explained, "Giant stumps like bleached skeletons littered
the landscape, which supported no trees beyond a few inches in diameter.
With much of the forest destroyed and ground cover burned, floods became frequent and large, and . . . sudden flows [caused] year-round river
levels [to fall] sharply. Pine seed supplies declined and white pine blister
rust arrived to attack younger trees, opening the way invasion and prolif-
eration of other species, especially aspen."[24]

Economist Frederick Merk wrote in 1916, "In every new country the
natural resources closest at hand are the first to be exploited. . . . The gifts
of nature are transformed into capital as rapidly as possible, and the means

A section of cutover land further devastated by fire and soil erosion. WHI IMAGE ID 3991

thus accumulated form the basis for the development of other fields of industry. In Wisconsin lumber was one of the easiest to transmute the great northern forests into gold. . . . With reckless disregard for the future they wasted the gift of the ages."[25]

Even before the mass harvesting of Wisconsin's white pine had ended, the logging companies had begun adjusting to the demise of their prime timber resource. As early as 1876, the demand for hardwoods had grown substantially. In fact, by the early 1890s, some sawmills were cutting only hardwoods. By 1899, the hardwood and hemlock cut reached about 900 million board feet. Some significant logging companies moved out of the state, looking elsewhere for trees to cut. Frederick Weyerhaeuser bought substantial acreages in the south and also looked to the West Coast for lumber prospects.[26]

After reaching its zenith in 1890, the state's lumber industry began a slow decline, partly due to the nationwide economic depression that began to take hold in 1893.[27] Wisconsin continued to rank among the top five states producing forest products for several more years. But by 1920, the state had slipped to number ten in the nation in lumber production. In 1930, forest industries had slipped to fourteenth among all of Wisconsin's industries. Interestingly, as Wisconsin's lumber production dropped, its production of pulpwood grew dramatically, as the state moved toward becoming the leading paper manufacturer in the nation.[28]

Much of northern Wisconsin had come to depend on logging and related enterprises. As historian Robert Fries wrote, the forest industry "built towns and cities, road, bridges, and railways. . . . It brought money as well as people from other states. It contributed a substantial share of the revenues required for the administration of state and local government."[29] But beginning in the early 1900s, a great quiet came over the Northwoods. There was no sound of the ax or the crosscut saw or logger's cry as yet another giant pine crashed to the ground, no scream of the sawmill saw slicing through logs and turning them into lumber. And in the spring, when the ice went out on the streams and rivers, all one heard was the murmuring of water running over rapids—no log drivers shouting to one another as they tried to steer the logs that tumbled over each other on their way to the sawmills. Left behind were acres upon acres of stumps, ghosts of what had been and would be no more. Most of the lumber companies had taken their money, jobs, and influence and moved on to other places where there were trees to cut and money to be made.

Towns and cities suffered when the lumber industry began drying up and people started leaving. The saloons were quiet on Saturday nights. The boarding houses were empty and the brothels boarded up. Many businesses posted Closed signs.

The population of Ashland County declined by 14 percent between 1920 and 1930. The population of Bayfield County, which had increased by nearly 1,200 percent during the 1880s, grew less than 8 percent from 1910 to 1920.[30] The great pinery was no more, and what remained were thousands of acres of denuded desolation. What would become of the Northwoods now that it was no longer the woods?

9

THE PLOW FOLLOWED
THE AX

By the early 1900s, the logging companies knew that the white pine woodlands were not the infinite, inexhaustible resource that some of them had believed. To avoid paying taxes on the land they owned, many either simply abandoned their property or tried to sell their vast acreages to farmers. A few companies held on to their land and began practicing what we would now call sustainable forestry. The Goodman and Connor companies, for example, saw a future in selective cutting of their forestland. But many did not, choosing instead to cut and run.

The cutover left behind when the loggers moved on included large swaths of Oconto, Marinette, Langlade, Forest, and Florence Counties in northeastern Wisconsin; Lincoln, Oneida, Vilas, Iron, Price, Ashland, and Taylor Counties in northcentral Wisconsin; and Rusk, Sawyer, Bayfield, Douglas, Washburn, and Burnett Counties in northwestern Wisconsin.[1]

Once logging operations ceased in Wisconsin's northern counties, the logging companies disposed of the cutover lands primarily in one of three ways: selling the land to a buyer directly, pooling it with land owned by other companies for sale by a consortium, or selling it to a middleman. Many land deals with varying financial structures resulted. The J. L. Gates Land Company, with finances from Milwaukee's Pfister family, sold hundreds of acres of cutover land to farm families enticed to move there from Chicago and Milwaukee. The Wisconsin Central Railroad, working with a European agent, sold cutover land in central Wisconsin to five thousand Germans.[2]

The Daniel Shaw Lumber Company owned thousands of acres in the Chippewa River Valley. After several failed attempts at land sales, the company began working with the Gates Land Company to assemble cutover land for sale to farmers. New York's Cornell University, once the recipient of bounteous pinery land thanks to the federal land grants of 1862, now found itself the owner of thousands of acres of cutover land. It transferred 50,000 of its unsold acres to the Gates Land Company. Overall, between 1898 and 1902, Gates sold 456,000 acres of cutover land.[3]

Trying to find some use for the cutover lands and get more acres on the tax rolls, in 1895, the Wisconsin legislature created a State Board of Immigration, to be overseen by a secretary with an office in Rhinelander. The law provided funds for a promotional publication to be prepared under the direction of the University of Wisconsin's dean of agriculture, William Henry. Professors Henry, F. H. King, and E. S. Goff traveled throughout the northern cutover counties to assess the soil, consider the kinds of crops that might do well in the north, and determine the potential for livestock production, dairying, sheep raising, and fruit growing. The area they surveyed was above an imaginary line drawn from Green Bay to Hudson.

Their survey resulted in the publication of *Northern Wisconsin: A Handbook for the Home Seeker* in 1896. In it, Dean Henry wrote, "With farms supplanting the forest, northern Wisconsin will not revert to a wilderness with the passing of the lumber industry but will be occupied by a thrifty class of farmers whose well-directed, intelligent efforts bring substantial, satisfactory returns from fields, flocks and herds."[4] The book contained an assortment of photos depicting abundant crops, healthy livestock, and successful farm families. It was designed to promote farming as an economic activity to replace the millions of board feet the logging companies had removed from the northern region of the state.

In 1897, just two years after Dean Henry and his colleagues conducted their survey of the agricultural potential in the northern counties, the Wisconsin Geological and Natural History Survey sent Filbert Roth to conduct a study of the soils of northern Wisconsin counties and their potential for farming. Roth's report revealed that much of the area was covered by grayish clay and loam soils but that rather poor sandy soils made up about 15 percent of the total area. He wrote, "It would appear that about 20 percent of the area is good farmland, about 40 percent medium, while

The photographs in *Northern Wisconsin: A Handbook for the Home Seeker* were meant to entice farmers to the cutover land. The caption that ran with this one, taken in Price County, read, "This view was taken after this family took up its residence, November 1st, 1896. They were without means, but from work getting out timber from the land, they will live in comfort during the winter and have a nice clearing for crops in the spring." WHI IMAGE ID 94063

The *Handbook* promised bountiful crops, like this pile of potatoes reported to have weighed 174 pounds. WHI IMAGE ID 93246

nearly 40 percent is either not at all suited to farming or only doubtfully so and should, by all means, be left to forest."[5]

Few paid any attention to the fact that in much of the north, the land had little potential for farming. In addition, the length of the growing season—the number of frost-free days in Antigo in northern Wisconsin, for example, is about 119 days, whereas in Madison, it is about 157 days—made growing many crops in the north a challenge.

The State Board of Immigration distributed the handbook widely throughout Europe and Canada, and by 1920, thousands of immigrants had moved into the cutover and taken up farming. The majority of them were Norwegians, Swedes, Finns, and Danes, plus some Germans, Poles, and Canadians. Historian Joseph Shafer wrote in 1922, "Those who have accustomed themselves to think of northern Wisconsin as a vast, undeveloped woodland, and have failed to keep up with the statistics of growth or to view the country at first hand, will be quite unprepared to appreciate the results of agricultural history in that region. . . . In the region are some of the finest farms in the state with modern buildings, the best improved or purebred stock, and well tilled fields growing splendid crops of hay, grain, and silage corn."[6]

As the settlers arrived in the cutover, they almost immediately wanted roads and schools, and they expected that the county governments would cover the cost. County governments levied taxes on all landowners and did not differentiate between land that was logged and that which was not. The logging companies became even more eager to sell their cutover land, both to use the income to purchase new tracts of unlogged forestland and to avoid the taxes.[7]

In Suamico, after the timber resources were depleted and the sawmills closed, former mill workers bought some of the land, intent on farming. According to a history of the town, "As soon as the new settlers had a home for themselves and a small shed or barn, the entire family set to work clearing the land. . . . The people worked hard, even hauling marsh hay from the bay shore [Green Bay] about five miles away to feed the livestock until enough land could be cleared to raise the feed."[8]

The Goodman Lumber Company, operating in Marinette and nearby counties, planned to sell its cutover timberland to farmers. To help would-be farmers see a cutover farm in action, the company started an eighty-acre model farm. By 1910, the Goodman company had cleared about twenty acres of stumps. Milk produced by the farm met the needs of the village of Goodman, and its crops fed the logging camps that the company continued to operate. The Goodman Lumber Company also sold about seven thousand acres of its cutover land to the Slavic Land Association of Chicago for six dollars per acre. The plan was for some eighty to one hundred Bohemian families to create an agricultural colony and raise potatoes as a primary crop.[9] The record does not reveal whether the plan succeeded.

In 1890, some two hundred thousand acres in northern Wisconsin was opened to settlement under provisions of the Homestead Act of 1862. This Water Reserve Land had been set aside by the federal government in 1880 and 1881 "for the reason that such lands would be required for or subject to flowage in the construction of dams, reservoirs, and other works for the improvement of navigation of the Mississippi and certain of its tributaries."[10] An area newspaper reported the following:

> The Water Reserve Land was opened for homestead on the 20th, last Saturday. Thousands of people hastened to the Wausau land office as early as Thursday and Friday, and thousands came away disappointed, not so much for the fact that they didn't get a homestead, as over the way the Wausau people managed the business. Outsiders knew that it was a chance game, but they thought all would be treated alike. Wausau men were shown all the favoritism that was needed for them to secure all choice tracts of the reserve land. Three-fourths of the claims that were taken were by residents of Wausau, and if an outsider got a filing it was on something Wausau people didn't want.[11]

As a result of this and other promotions, several thousand settlers came to the vast cutover region, many buying forty or eighty acres. While the average acre of farmland in 1900 sold for about twenty-seven dollars an acre, cutover land was going for just eight to ten dollars an acre.[12]

Logging company land sales continued for many years. In 1926, according to a Rhinelander news report,

> One of the biggest land deals completed in northern Wisconsin within the past five years was announced yesterday at Merrill. It involves the

sale of some 13,000 acres of lake country land representing the total
holdings of the Vilas County Lumber Company, formerly located at
Winegar [now Presque Isle]. That company finished its operations last
year and removed a heavy cover of pine, hemlock, and hardwood, but
considerable areas of the tract are still well wooded and there is abundant timber and material for construction of summer homes, cot-
tages, and resort buildings.

Richard B. Runke, of Merrill, and associates purchased the land
which has an actual lake frontage of more than 20 miles on 35 lakes
along the Wisconsin-Michigan state line. Of these lakes, 17 are entirely included in the tract.[13]

Settlers wishing to farm this vast area denuded of its timber resources
faced many challenges, with stump removal topping the list. The loggers
had left behind thousands of acres of pine stumps, many standing three or
four feet high and up to four feet in diameter, with an extensive, spreading
root system. Oneida County was estimated to have on average 117 stumps
per acre.[14]

Assisting settlers in the cutover with stump removal was one of the
early tasks of the new University of Wisconsin College of Agriculture
county agents. The first county agent in Wisconsin, E. L. Luther, began
work in Oneida County in 1912. In 1916, the College of Agriculture, in cooperation with railroad companies sent "land clearing trains" across northern Wisconsin. At each stop, university specialists spoke to the gathered
crowd about everything from how to make a mechanical stump puller to
how to blast them with dynamite.[15]

By 1920, nearly all of northern Wisconsin counties employed county
agents. The agents working in the cutover counties faced three significant
challenges: convincing people living on a cutover farm that their future
success as farmers depended on land clearing, helping farmers obtain
the materials needed for land clearing, and using land-clearing materials
safely and with maximum return at minimum cost.[16]

Various types of stump pullers powered by a team of horses were some-
what successful, but the work was time consuming. Blasting a stump, albeit
considerably more dangerous, was quicker and more effective than any
of the mechanical stump pullers. Luckily, the United States government

BLOWING UP STUMPS

Gale VandeBerg, now in his nineties, recalled helping his father blow up stumps on the home farm in Clark County, which his father had purchased in 1913. During the 1920s and 1930s, the VandeBergs spent considerable time every year clearing yet another few acres of land. The necessary blasting supplies, VandeBerg recalled, "included boxes of dynamite caps, fuses, boxes filled with sticks of dynamite, a short auger for making holes and an auger some four feet long for reaching under the stump. A stick of dynamite is like a giant firecracker, some eight inches long and 1½ inches in diameter."

VandeBerg remembered his father as an excellent dynamite blaster:

I would watch as he augered the holes at certain angles and at various depths. Depending upon the size of the stump, he might set one, two, or even three charges [dynamite sticks] in different places under the stump. Then he would cut and toggle the fuses and caps in such a way that they would all go off simultaneously. He would send me off, perhaps 200 feet, and tell me to hold my hands over my ears. . . . He would pull from his overalls pocket a big wooden sulfur-match, light it by scratching it along on his outstretched hind quarter, light the fuse and then trot off for his own protection. You could hear the sizzle as the fuse burned its way slowly to the charges and then—BOOM-M-M! The great blast would shake the very earth I was standing on and sometimes even the windows of our house more than a quarter mile away. The giant stump and surrounding dirt went exploding skyward, scattering debris and pieces of the stump in a circle of 100 feet in diameter. Some of the big pine stump roots were left partially sticking out of the ground. To these, we would later fasten a logging chain and pull them out with the horses.

Note

Gale VandeBerg, "Land Clearing—Dynamite Blasting," in *And That's the Way It Was: 55 Stories of Farming and Rural Living in Wisconsin, 1880–1943* (Madison, WI: self-pub., 2001).

A University of Wisconsin College of Agriculture team ready to educate farmers about the safe use of explosives for stump removal. WHI IMAGE ID 7147

had several million pounds of TNT it no longer needed after the signing of the World War I armistice. Wisconsin Congressman A. P. Nelson obtained two hundred thousand pounds of TNT for use in Wisconsin land-clearing projects. The College of Agriculture specialists conducted TNT demonstrations for some five thousand farmers from fifteen northern Wisconsin counties.[17]

In addition, in 1921 the federal government allotted Wisconsin seven hundred thousand pounds of the explosive picric acid, also left over from World War I. The explosive was distributed to farmers for the cost of putting it in cartridges plus packing and shipping. By 1922, settlers in the cutover had cleared some 135,000 acres of land.[18]

Walter Rowlands gained experience working with explosives when he served in the Canadian Army. The College of Agriculture's Agricultural Engineering Department hired Rowlands in 1923 to lead its land-clearing program. Rowlands had worked as an extension agent for a short time in Marinette County, where he saw the cutover first hand. John Swenehart, another former extension agent, was hired by the Agricultural Engineering Department to assist him. Rowlands and Swenehart traveled across the northern Wisconsin counties, conducting demonstrations on the safe use of former military explosives for land clearing. Using explosives for stump removal was a dangerous business. There are many stories of farmers attempting to blast stumps and losing limbs or even their lives when an explosive did not respond as planned.

As early as the 1920s, it was clear to Wisconsin lawmakers, lumber interests, and many of the farmers themselves that much of the former timberland in northern Wisconsin was best suited for forestry, not farming. Much of the cutover soil was too sandy, and the short growing season prevented certain crops, such as corn, from maturing before frost killed the plant. Some farmers stayed on their poor farms, but many did not. Between 1920 and 1930, the population of Wisconsin increased by 11.7 percent. But in the cutover region, the population decreased from 322,000 to 314,000. There were exceptions: counties on the southern edge of the great pinery, including Brown, Shawano, Waupaca, Portage, Wood, Marathon, Jackson, Eau Claire, Dunn, Saint Croix, Buffalo, and Polk, had seen considerable logging, but they were better suited to farming than were those farther north.[19]

Blowing up a stump, 1921.
WHI IMAGE ID 78988

In that decade, tax delinquency spread across the northern cutover as farmers packed up and left, abandoning their land for others to worry about. In Forest County, deep in the cutover, 43 percent of the total acreage had left the tax base by 1938. The Great Depression of the 1930s further devastated the cutover farms, reducing the average cutover farm's income by 40 percent between the 1920s and 1939. The harsh economic realities of the 1930s ended the hopes of many farmers trying to make a living in the cutover.[20]

10

REFORESTATION
EFFORTS

In the early 1900s, many of Wisconsin's decision makers continued to promote the vast acreage of cutover lands as having high potential for farming. They also believed that some of the former pineland would restore itself by self-seeding. But Filbert Roth's 1897 survey of the pinery suggested otherwise. Writing about the potential for white pine to return to the logged regions without any outside effort, Roth said, "While the ability of white pine to reproduce itself is thus amply demonstrated in every county in North Wisconsin, the fact remains that the great body of cut-over pinelands have not and do not at present recover themselves with young pine, but that more than 80 percent of the bare, burned, cut-over lands are practically devoid of any valuable forest growth whatever."[1]

Something else had to be done with those lands where farming was not possible and where self-seeding was not happening. On some cut-over lands, huge gullies formed because there was nothing to slow down a heavy rain. With slashings still abundant, fire continued to be a threat. And from an aesthetic perspective, the cutover region was depressingly devoid of any beauty.

It was not until six years after Roth's study, in 1903, that the Wisconsin legislature passed a comprehensive forestry law. Provisions of the law included creating a Department of State Forestry to be controlled by a Board of State Forest Commissioners, creating the position of state superintendent of forests (later called state forester), creating forest experiment stations, allowing the state to accept grants of land for forestry purposes, establishing a system of state forests, providing for the disposition of public lands, and setting aside sixty-two thousand acres in Forest, Oneida, Vilas, and Iron Counties as a forest reserve.[2] The next year, US Senator Robert M. La Follette introduced legislation that allowed Wisconsin to acquire twenty thousand acres of vacant land from the federal government for forestry purposes.[3]

Wisconsin hired its first forester, Edward Merriam Griffith, on February 8, 1904. Thirty-two years old and a native of Brooklyn, New York, Griffith had attended Yale as an engineering student and studied forestry during his senior year in Germany. In 1898, Gifford Pinchot was hired as chief of forest service in the US Department of Agriculture and hired Griffith to promote better management of the nation's national forests. In his new role as Wisconsin's state forester, Griffith immediately began developing a series of programs including forest fire control, acquisition of land for the state forest reserve, and educational courses at the University of Wisconsin on forestry topics. Griffith also promoted the idea that forests had powerful influence on streams and rivers by helping stabilize stream flow and slowing down snowmelt in spring.[4]

In 1905, the Wisconsin legislature took up the question of the state's forests once more. Chapter 264 of the Laws of 1905 included the following:

- The creation of a State Board of Forestry "consisting of the president of the state university, the director of the state geological survey, the dean of the state agricultural department, the attorney-general and one other member to be appointed by the governor."

- Changing the title of the state superintendent of forests to state forester and adding the requirement that the person in the role be a trained forester. The state forester would also be the state fire warden and would direct, under the supervision of the state board of forestry, the management of the state forest reserve.

- Creating the position of assistant state forester.

- Ceasing selling forest reserve lands owned by the state north of township 33 north and designating those lands the state forest reserve.[5]

The state forest reserve nursery at Trout Lake, 1911. WHI IMAGE ID 107609

From 1911 to 1915, through Griffith's efforts, Wisconsin added 183,000 acres to the public forest reserve. In 1911, Wisconsin developed its first tree nursery at Trout Lake in Vilas County. The state purchased 192,000 conifer seedlings from Michigan in 1911 and another 18,000 seedlings in 1912 to be planted at Trout Lake.[6]

In 1913, 68,500 trees that had been grown at the new nursery were planted on state forestlands. A year later, with the expansion of the Trout Lake nursery, a half million trees were planted. By 1915, Wisconsin had seen real progress in tree planting and reclaimed many acres of the former cutover as forestland. With State Forester Griffith's leadership, it appeared Wisconsin was well on its way to developing a long-range plan for the cutover region and to carrying out much of that plan through land acquisition and planting programs.

But not everyone was happy. Opposition to the reclamation efforts on the part of lumber interests and northern Wisconsin legislators led to the appointment of a special legislative committee in 1915. Ultimately, the State Supreme Court ruled that Wisconsin laws regarding forestry and the use of state funds to purchase forest reserve land was illegal. A disappointed and dismayed Edward Griffith left Wisconsin in 1917.[7]

With the 1915 Supreme Court decision, it appeared that the state of Wisconsin's direct involvement in reforestation was dead. It would be almost ten years before the public's interest in reforestation with state support resumed. Meanwhile, the years 1915 to 1920 saw continued encouragement from the state, including through the University of Wisconsin's College of Agriculture, to attract farmers to the cutover lands. The work of Griffith and other forestry leaders who had advocated saving large swaths of the cutover for reforestation was dismissed or simply ignored. World War I saw a sharp increase in food prices, making farming financially possible even on marginal land, and after the war, the cutover land was also seen as a place for war veterans to farm and raise families. Nevertheless, the number of settlers in the region decreased from 1921 to 1925. Rather than achieving a once-in-a-lifetime dream of owning a thriving farm, these cutover settlers had become the subjects of what felt like a cruel hoax.[8]

Meanwhile, by the mid-1920s, lumber and paper companies began getting into the business of cutover reforestation to assure they would have wood products for their operations in the future. The Consolidated Water Power and Paper Company of Wisconsin Rapids planted seedlings on cutover land near Biron in 1923. The Connor Lumber and Land Company of Laona began an extensive reforestation program in the cutover region; acquiring trees from the Trout Lake Nursery, the company planted fifty thousand red and white pine in 1928, with plans to plant one hundred thousand seedlings in 1929. In 1925 and 1926, the Nekoosa-Edwards Paper Company planted some one hundred thousand jack and red pine seedlings on land near Port Edwards and Nekoosa. These various plantings were the start of what became known as industrial forestry.[9]

In 1924, an amendment identical to the law that in 1915 had been declared unconstitutional by the Wisconsin Supreme Court was approved by an overwhelming majority of Wisconsin voters. After several fits and starts, Wisconsin citizens had again approved the need for the state to assist in the reforestation of the north. More than one million trees were distributed and planted in 1926.[10]

In Wisconsin, title to land where taxes are not paid reverts to the counties. But in the early 1920s, many of the counties did not want this tax-delinquent land because they had no legal authority to manage it. Furthermore, having large acreages of once "promising" farmland taken off the tax rolls reduced the county's tax base and reduced its ability to carry out routine government functions, such as providing schools and roads.

In 1925, Wisconsin's legislature, recognizing the growing problem with cutover lands, passed the uniform tax clause of the state constitution. Its passage resulted in the Forest Crop Law of 1927. The law included the following provisions: A property owner with 160 or more acres (later reduced to 40 acres) could declare his or her land best suited for forestry. The owner would sign a fifty-year renewable contract with the state. Other than a fee of ten cents per acre, the owner paid no property taxes. To aid the municipalities, the state paid them ten cents per acre for all lands in the forest crop program. (By the end of 1986, the Forest Crop Law program had enrolled about a million and half acres of private forestland. The Managed Forest Law [MFL] succeeded the Forest Crop Law in 1986. In 2017, more than three million acres of private forestland were enrolled under the MFL).[11]

The theme at Wisconsin's first commercial forestry conference, held in Milwaukee in March 1928, was "the treatment of timber as an agricultural crop grown for profit and the application of biological science in the development of merchantable timber products, as presented at this conference, awakening a general and practical interest and [demonstrating] that forestry has a general as well as a sentimental basis."[12] The conference was a clear indication that Wisconsin forestry experts, government officials, the University of Wisconsin College of Agriculture, and industry leaders saw that northern Wisconsin was in trouble. Tens of thousands of acres, once studded with majestic pine trees, now appeared to be a forgotten wasteland.

The conference featured speakers from the University of Wisconsin, the forest products industry, the paper industry, the press, and the US Forest Service, along with the secretary of the US Department of Agriculture and private forest owners. Their topics included "The Land and Forest Situation in Wisconsin," "What Forests Mean," "Forestry by Private Owners," "Fire Control in Wisconsin," "The Forest Crop Law," "Forest Utilization," and more. Some seventy people attended.

Conference chair and papermill owner D. C. Everest later summarized the conference findings in an official report, highlighting these conclusions:

1. An inventory of the forest resources in Wisconsin is necessary.

2. These northern Wisconsin land resources should be classified into three categories—those best suited for agriculture, those for recreation, and those for forestry.[13]

In his closing comments, Everest said, "We have learned that [Wisconsin's forestry problem] cannot be solved quickly; that every group of lands, every individual ownership, every project which is to be considered as a potential forestry resource must be studied carefully and a program outlined for that particular set up. Individuals and corporations intending to carry on forestry as a business will do well to make haste slowly."[14]

The conference's resolution committee made these recommendations:

1. There should be increased tree planting especially on lands denuded of trees.

2. Fire protection should be available for all forestland.

3. Forest research must continue.

4. Counties with tax-delinquent forestland should practice reforestation on these acres.

5. School forests should be encouraged.

6. A land economy survey of the north should be taken.[15]

By 1931, the country was well into the Great Depression, and a subcommittee of Governor Phillip La Follette's Committee on Land Use and Forestry was asked to study the need for additional reforestation efforts. The committee's 1932 report recommended that the state "commence at once a forest planting program on suitable lands to sustain the industry, to afford employment, and to keep land best suited for such use in productive condition." With these new marching orders, it quickly became evident that the state needed an additional tree nursery in central Wisconsin. An area three miles south of Wisconsin Rapids was selected as the site, and the new nursery, known as the Griffith Nursery, began operations in 1932. In 1934, the Griffith Nursery distributed more than 16.5 million trees. By the

A view of the Griffith Nursery showing rows of seedlings and an above-ground irrigation system. WHI IMAGE ID 132009

late 1930s, the Griffith Nursery had expanded to three times its original size. Improvements were also made to the Trout Lake Nursery, and an additional nursery was established near Gordon in Douglas County, all with the help of workers in the Civilian Conservation Corps.[16]

THE CIVILIAN CONSERVATION CORPS

As unemployment was soaring during the Great Depression, President Franklin D. Roosevelt, with the help of Congress, created the Civilian Conservation Corps (CCC) in 1933. By 1938, forty-five CCC camps operated in Wisconsin; thirteen of them were devoted to soil conservation and were guided by the federal Soil Conservation Service. Soil Conservation Service camps included those at West Salem, Onalaska, Glen Haven, Nelson, Argyle, Platteville, and Coon Valley. Workers at these camps constructed terraces, worked on drainage control, and planted trees, including creating windbreaks.[1]

(continued)

Twelve camps were located in Wisconsin's national forests with fire-fighting, tree planting, and other such activities their primary work. These camps' activities were directed by representatives of the US Forest Service, and most were located in northern counties, including camps at Florence, Laona, Drummond, Park Falls, and Three Lakes. Twelve other CCC camps were based in Wisconsin state forests, where they carried out duties similar to those performed in the national parks. Eight camps operated in Wisconsin state parks, where they constructed buildings, built roads, and made other park improvements.[2]

Civilian Conservation Corps workers plant trees in the American Legion State Forest, Oneida County, 1936.
WHI IMAGE ID 131500

In 1933, Wisconsin CCC boys planted more than two million trees in county forests. In 1940, that number soared to 25 million trees planted on county forestland. After World War II started in 1941, the CCC closed down, and thousands of former CCC boys were off to war. The number of trees planted in county forests plummeted. But the CCC had a lasting impact on Wisconsin, both enhancing the state's natural resources and saving a generation of young men who had lost work and hope during the Great Depression.[3]

Notes

1. Jerry Apps, *The Civilian Conservation Corps in Wisconsin: Nature's Army at Work* (Madison: Wisconsin Historical Society Press, 2019).
2. Paul W. Glad, *War, a New Era, and Depression, 1914–1940*, The History of Wisconsin, vol. 5 (Madison: State Historical Society of Wisconsin, 1990), 494.
3. Jeremiah J. Auer, "A Century of Tree Planting: Wisconsin's Forestry Nursery System," *Tree Planters' Notes* 54, no. 2 (2011): 23–29.

Zoning Laws

In the late 1920s, to prevent another debacle of farmers settling on land not suited for farming and building under the Forest Crop Law of 1927, a movement began to promote rural zoning in the cutover counties. Several northern Wisconsin counties passed county zoning laws with the stated purpose to "discourage the farming of sub-marginal land, to separate the forest and recreational land from the farmland. . . . Land in the Forestry district may be used for forestry and forest-connected industries, the harvesting of wild crops, and recreational activities, including part-time residence. Agriculture is prohibited, as is year-around residence."[17]

In 1930, Professor Walter Rowlands, now of the University of Wisconsin College of Agriculture, accepted the position of extension district director, supervising the county agents who worked in the northern counties. According to a history of the college's agricultural engineering department, the Great Depression years in northern Wisconsin were "aggravated by the depletion of merchantable timber through cutting and fires, the collapse of supporting and related industries, and the limitations of agricultural production caused by short growing seasons, soils poorly adapted to agriculture, and an influx of inexperienced settlers."[18]

Working with forestry professor Fred Trenk, Rowlands met with county boards to help them develop zoning ordinances to prevent settlers from failing as farmers and not paying their taxes. Trenk and Rowlands met many times in each of the twenty-four counties in the north and prepared township maps to show land ownership, roads, and schools and indicate where the best lands for farming were located. In 1933, Oneida was the first county to adopt a zoning ordinance. By the end of 1935, all of the twenty-four northern counties except Taylor had done so. Taylor County's zoning ordinance was passed in 1937.[19]

Once the zoning was completed, the next task was to convince settlers trying to farm in remote areas with poor farming potential to swap their land for acres more suited to farming but still owned by the government. University of Wisconsin county agents led the educational effort to move farmers from poor agricultural land and, along with local governmental officials, to encourage reforestation of reclaimed acres. Marinette was the first county to attempt the resettlement of farmers from remote farms with soil unsuitable for farming to land better suited. The county agent, C. B. Drewry, worked with the farmers, some of whom sold their lands and others who made exchanges. Marinette County purchased sixteen farms totaling 1,120 acres between 1936 and 1944.

The federal government's Northern Wisconsin Settler Relocation Project provided funds to buy these farms. About four hundred farms in seven cutover counties were purchased.[20]

County, State, and National Forests

In 1927, the same year the Forest Crop Law was passed, the Wisconsin legislature passed a law commonly known as the County Forest Reserve Law, which allowed counties to establish county forests, often using tax-delinquent lands for that purpose. The law stated: "The people of any county may at any general election authorize the county board to acquire land by tax deed or otherwise for the purpose of establishing a county forest reserve."[21] County forests represent the state's largest publicly owned forestland; by 2017, twenty-nine of Wisconsin's seventy-two counties had county forests, totaling more than 2.36 million acres. The first Wisconsin county forest was established in Langlade County in 1928.[22]

Wisconsin's first state forest began with a gift from one of Wisconsin's prominent loggers, Frederick Weyerhaeuser. In 1907, Weyerhaeuser deeded 2,840 acres of northern Wisconsin forestland to the state of Wisconsin, creating the Brule River State Forest. Later grants from the federal government and purchases from private individuals and Douglas County increased the forest's size to 3,523 acres. One hundred years after the forest's creation, it received nearly 6,000 additional acres of land from a collaboration of the Wausau Paper Mills, the Warren Knowles–Gaylord Nelson Stewardship Fund, and the Wisconsin Conservation Fund. With previous land acquisitions, total acreage for the forest reached nearly 47,000 acres. Today Wisconsin has nine state forests covering more than 470,000 acres:

Black River State Forest: 68,706 acres
Brule River State Forest: 46,667 acres
Coulee Experimental Forest: 2,944 acres

Flambeau River State Forest: 89,975 acres
Governor Knowles State Forest: 20,614 acres
Northern Highland–American Legion State Forest: 234,366 acres
Kettle Moraine State Forest (northern unit): 30,041 acres
Kettle Moraine State Forest (southern unit): 21,315 acres
Peshtigo River State Forest: 9,403 acres
Point Beach State Forest: 2,917 acres[23]

A group of teens get to know the trees in the Kettle Moraine State Forest, 1939.
WHI IMAGE ID 132613

Counties that became the owner of tax-delinquent acres could in turn sell the land to the federal government. This was the case with the land that is now Wisconsin's Chequamegon and Nicolet National Forests. Crossing twelve counties and comprising about a million and a half acres, Wisconsin's two national forests have been managed as one since 1993 and are now known as the Chequamegon–Nicolet National Forest. The Chequamegon portion of the forest includes 858,400 acres in Ashland, Bayfield, Sawyer, Price, Taylor, and Vilas Counties. The Nicolet portion includes about 661,400 acres in Florence, Forest, Langlade, Oconto, Oneida, and Vilas Counties.[24]

School Forests

In 1925, Dean Russell of the University of Wisconsin's College of Agriculture visited Australia and saw children planting trees on public land as an educational project. He immediately thought about the many acres of cutover lands in northern Wisconsin and considered whether this might be a way to reclaim some of that stump-strewn, burned-over land with "shovel and seedling." Wisconsin's state 4-H leader, Wakelin "Ranger Mac" McNeel, also began promoting school forests in the 1920s; he saw them as a way to help young people become active conservationists as well as contribute to the reclamation of cutover lands.

Dean Russell went to the state legislature with a plan that would permit school districts to own land for forestry programs.[25] With the passage of school forest legislation in 1927, McNeel and his colleague University of Wisconsin Extension Forester Fred Trenk immediately began working with school districts and county governments to encourage the development of school forests. By 1928, three tracts of land had been donated or purchased for school forests in Laona, Crandon, and Wabeno, all in the cutover region. The three school forests were dedicated in spring 1928.

The school forest movement received a boost in 1935 when Wisconsin's legislature passed a law mandating that conservation education be taught in all public high schools, vocational schools and universities, and colleges. A school forest provided an excellent site for conservation education activities. In 1949, Wisconsin legislators passed a law making free planting stock available from the state tree nurseries for planting in school forests.[26] Today, there are more than three hundred school forests in Wisconsin.

WILD ROSE SCHOOL FOREST

The Wild Rose School District purchased the first of three parcels of land that comprise the Wild Rose School Forest for one dollar from Harold and Ruth Fix on December 1, 1950. The land—138.8 acres valued at the time at five hundred dollars—is located in the township of Rose in Waushara County. In spring 1951, students from the Wild Rose School District began planting pine trees by hand on the land. I was part of the planting crew, along with my fellow high school seniors Douglas Jenks, David Jones, Jerry Stewart, Kenny Owens, Alan Walters, Eddie Schmidt, Carol Towne, Joan Nordahl, Barbara Radloff, and Patty Etheridge and students from several other grades.

The Wild Rose School District purchased the second segment, 39.644 acres in the town of Belmont and called the Frater Forest, on July 15, 1958. At the time, the property was valued at $392. The district purchased the third segment, 17.794 acres in Springwater Township in Waushara County, on December 27, 1985, for one dollar (valued at $15,300 at the time). Previous owners Otto J. and Meliva I. Keller stipulated that the acres be used only as a nature preserve. In 1992, the school district constructed a shelter house at the Keller property to make classroom field trip visits more convenient.

The school district practiced selective harvesting, meaning they thinned trees and cut only those of marketable size, in 1985 to 1989 and from 1991 to 1992. The most recent harvest was in 2006 to 2008 in the town of Rose and town of Belmont forests; it brought in $125,000 for the district.

In 2010, the school district, using earnings from timber sales, began offering scholarships to Wild Rose graduates interested in pursuing degrees in forestry and agriculture. Timber sales also fund trips for students attending environmental programs provided at the University of Wisconsin–Stevens Point's Environmental Station and at Trees for Tomorrow near Eagle River, Wisconsin.

Note
Craig Hayes, district administrator, and Diane Mrkvicka, business administrator, School District of Wild Rose, personal correspondence, November 20, 2017.

The Madison Metropolitan School District has had a school forest since 1959. The 287-acre forest is about twelve miles southwest of Madison in Wisconsin's Driftless Area. The school forest acreage includes valleys, steep ridges, 166 acres of oak woods, a conifer plantation planted by Madison schoolchildren, and open fields and sandstone rock outcrops.

According to the Madison Metropolitan School District School Forest Education Plan, a variety of experiences in the school forest teach students that

1. Humans are part of the natural world.
2. We rely on our environment for resources, recreation, and inspiration. Our lives are greatly influenced monetarily, recreationally, emotionally and spiritually by the natural resources in the Madison School Forest.
3. The natural world has inherent value.
4. We have an obligation to be good environmental stewards for the current and future health of the land and of humans. Environmental Stewardship, sustainability, and conservation are essential for ensuring a high quality of life for future generations on a local, regional, national and global scale.
5. Knowledge and skills will allow students to make informed choices and develop lifestyles that contribute to a healthy society and environment.
6. Taking an active role in responsible resource use will help to sustain and improve our environment and community.
7. Responsible citizens will act wisely regarding the overall health of the environment.[27]

SHELTERBELTS

The Great Depression of the 1930s affected almost everyone, whether they lived on farms or in cities. The weather during those years also contributed to the country's problems. Wicked dust storms raged in the country's Southwest, tearing up farmland and upending the lives of thousands who sought relief from the dust-filled, raging winds. Wisconsin was not spared from the dust storms, particularly in the Central Sands region of Waushara, Adams, Marquette, Wood, and Portage Counties.

Shelterbelts helped ameliorate the problem. Trees planted along the edges of fields slowed down the winds and prevented sandy soils from blowing away. County extension agents' offices and local soil conservation technicians worked together to conduct surveys to determine the tree requirements for shelterbelts in the central counties. The state Conservation Department provided more than 14 million trees, mostly transplants, from 1924 to 1944. Farmers in the affected counties were asked to sign an agreement saying they would plant the trees as instructed. The trees were planted in three-row shelterbelts. It was estimated that by 1944, some 5,492 miles of shelterbelts had been planted. For the most part, shelterbelts were highly effective, especially in the flat, sandy regions of the state, such as in central Wisconsin, where the winds had a clear sweep.[28]

By the early 1900s, much of what had once been beautiful forested land in northern Wisconsin had been decimated. At first, Wisconsin government and university officials advocated for farming in the area, going so far as to promote—with considerable exaggeration—the cutover's agricultural attributes. But after realizing that farming was not the answer for the north, Wisconsin lawmakers, academics, and forest industry experts turned to a plan for reforestation. Thanks to those efforts and the work of the Civilian Conservation Corps, the barren cutover land was converted once again to thriving forests.

EPILOGUE

Over the half-century from 1860 to 1910, logging, lumber production, and affiliated enterprises provided jobs for tens of thousands of Wisconsinites and great wealth for many individuals. The industry touched the lives of nearly every Wisconsin citizen, from an immigrant lumberjack or camp cook in the Chippewa Valley to a Suamico sawmill operator, an Oshkosh factory worker to a Milwaukee banker.

By its peak in the 1890s, the logging and lumber industry was an organized and industrial-scale enterprise focused on extracting the maximum financial gain from the available forest resources. The industry removed virtually all of Wisconsin's northern forests in the span of fifty years, leaving behind hundreds of square miles of stumps and slash. The northern forests and their loss and subsequent replacement have defined the economic prospects, physical surroundings, and community institutions for Wisconsin citizens ever since. The lessons learned in the pinery continue to shape the state today.

The days of lumberjacks spending the winter in remote and rustic Northwoods logging camps are far in the past. By the early 1950s, gasoline-powered chainsaws had replaced the crosscut saw in logging operations. (The first chainsaws were six-horsepower, 150-pound beasts that required two men to operate them.)[1] The mechanical chainsaw paved the way for a series of inventions that transformed the commercial logging industry. Now logging companies could send crews with chainsaws into the woods in all seasons of the year to cut trees, load them on trucks, and haul them to nearby sawmills. The lumberjacks generally lived at home with their families; some stayed in a motel near the worksite but headed home to spend weekends with their families.

In the 1980s, a new generation of logging equipment emerged that made the industry safer and more efficient. The forest harvester, used to cut down trees, remove branches, and cut the trees into uniform lengths, runs on huge rubber tires or on tracks and can navigate almost any woodlot. The operator sits inside the machine's cab, protected from not only the weather but also the dreaded mosquitos and deerflies that plagued the lumberjacks of earlier days. The forwarder follows the harvester and, with hydraulically operated arms, picks up the cut logs, loads them (as many as eight cords) on its back, and transports them to the landing area where they are piled to await the logging trucks. Of course, these highly efficient machines require a huge investment by the logging company: a modern harvester costs between $500,000 and $800,000; a forwarder costs between $250,000 and $400,000.[2]

Powerful modern equipment also leaves behind a trail of disturbed forest soil and downed limbs and brush. Today, the number of woodlot owners who prefer to use axes, chainsaws, and horses for their operations is growing. As a writer for *Farming Magazine* noted, "Using draft horses to manage forests and woodlots minimizes the damage left behind. . . . [It] also requires little investment in large tools or equipment."[3]

In 2019, of Wisconsin's 35 million acres of land, 17.1 million acres, or 49 percent, was forestland. (Urban forests accounted for an addition 2 million acres.) The majority of the state's forestland, 10.4 million acres, is owned by individuals and families; the rest is owned by corporations, the state and federal governments, local governments, and American Indian nations.[4] The predominant tree species in Wisconsin, in rank order, are sugar maple, red maple, northern red oak, eastern white pine, quaking

Tree harvester. PHOTO © STEVE APPS

Forwarder. PHOTO © STEVE APPS

aspen, red pine, American basswood, northern white cedar, white oak, and black ash. Interestingly, the famed white pine tree of Wisconsin's logging history is making a comeback in the state; from 2011 to 2016, white pine numbers increased by more than 17 percent.[5]

The wood products industries sparked by the logging and building booms of the middle to late 1800s continue to fuel the state's economy. The predominant product produced by Wisconsin's forests today is wood for the pulp and paper industry. Second is saw logs, used for furniture, flooring, cabinets, molding and millwork, posts, poles, and pilings. In 2019, Wisconsin's paper and pulp industry provided 30,262 jobs.[6] The value-added wood manufacturing industry, which includes sawmills and wood manufacturing plants, accounted for another 20,000 jobs.[7]

Wisconsin consulting forester Fred Hengst noted that while the market for some wood products has been unpredictable in recent years, certain markets, such as firewood, have grown. In another welcome change for woodlot owners, Hengst explained, "Certain species that were not able to be used for paper products in the past can now be used. . . . Oak used to be a less desirable pulpwood species due to difficulties in separating the cellulose, but the paper scientists improved the process for

This timber was harvested from the author's woodlot after a windstorm damaged many of the trees, requiring early harvesting. PHOTO © STEVE APPS

doing that."[8] According to the Wisconsin Council on Forestry, demand is growing overseas for Wisconsin's high-quality pulp and paper and wood for high-end furniture.[9]

While today's woodland owners must continually seek ways to run their operations more efficiently and economically, many of them are also highly motivated to use sustainable practices. The Wisconsin Department of Natural Resources defines sustainable forestry as "a holistic approach that aims to maintain forests as healthy ecosystems that will provide economic, ecological and social benefits for years to come. Keeping an ecosystem healthy includes management for wildlife habitat, aesthetics, soil and water quality, native biological diversity, recreational opportunities and forest products. Another important component of sustainable forestry is the periodic harvesting of trees."[10]

The Wisconsin Woodland Owners Association (WWOA), an organization of seventeen hundred private landowners, espouses those principles as well. Through education opportunities, field trips, and regional meetings, it provides its members support in the wise use and management of timber resources. As past WWOA president Steve Ring noted,

Economics are important, but sustainable practices should be the utmost goal of any timber sale. To stay on top of change, woodland owners must constantly educate themselves on the issues that may affect their forest. They should pick a professional forester or logger to work with. They should follow best management and sustainable practices, including applying practical information on dealing with invasive plants, disease control and learning best approaches for passing on their forests to the next generation. For the private woodland owner and the forest industry, sustainability must always be the number one goal when conducting a timber harvest. It not only protects our woodlands today but protects our woodlands for future generations to come.[11]

The Wisconsin forest industry is now facing new challenges. Some climate change researchers predict that between 2019 and 2050, Wisconsin's temperature will have warmed on average by six degrees Fahrenheit. Warming will be the greatest during the winter months, with increases of five to eleven degrees Fahrenheit by the middle of the twenty-first century. One result of warming temperatures is an increase in invasive species on forestland. Insects and diseases are likely to increase as well, along with the damage they can inflict. As average temperatures rise, cold-loving tree species such as sugar maple, black spruce, balsam fir, quaking aspen, and paper birch may decline.[12]

Climate change does offer some potential benefits. With a growing season that is extended by sixteen to thirty-two days, trees will have more time to grow. Some researchers believe that some tree species will grow faster with increased amounts of carbon dioxide in the atmosphere. This effect, known as CO_2 fertilization, will likely benefit hardwoods more than conifers. This unique kind of fertilization assumes adequate water and nutrients for the trees.[13]

═══

The forest industry has known many challenges since the first settlers arrived and discovered they had to clear the land of trees before they could plant a crop. Some of those challenges the industry brought on itself. Nevertheless, in 2017, Wisconsin's forest industry accounted for

13.5 percent of all jobs in the state, with about 64,000 employees in 1,207 paper and wood manufacturing businesses.[14] According to a 2019 report by the National Alliance of Forest Owners, in that year employment in Wisconsin forestry had grown by nearly 5 percent over 2010; the value of timber sales in the state grew by nearly 10 percent in the same period to $21.6 billion.[15]

Forests make up almost half of Wisconsin's landscape. They will continue to be one of the state's most important economic assets. In addition to the forest products made from its harvest, the Northwoods attracts thousands of tourists each year, contributing millions of dollars to the state's economy. In Oneida County alone, visitors spent $237.4 million in 2018.[16]

Of course, forests offer much more than financial opportunities. Our vast network of trees helps prevent soil and water erosion, provides habitat for birds and animals, and helps to mitigate the effects of climate change. The beauty of Wisconsin's forestland is unmatched, changing across the seasons, peaking in fall with an explosion of color. No matter the season, sitting in a forest, listening to the wind play in the tops of the trees, soothes the soul. Wisconsin would not be Wisconsin without its forests.

WISCONSIN LOGGING MUSEUMS

MENOMINEE LOGGING MUSEUM

Owned and operated by the Menominee Indian Tribe of Wisconsin, this comprehensive logging museum is located about one mile north of Keshena. The museum opened in 1968 after Dorothy and Jacque D. Vallier of Milwaukee donated their vast collection of lake states logging artifacts, including saws, axes, cant hooks, a log marking hammer, and even logging sleighs and a locomotive. They also donated money for the cost of labor and materials to construct the museum. For more information, visit www .menominee-nsn.gov.

PIONEER PARK HISTORICAL COMPLEX LOGGING MUSEUM, RHINELANDER

In 1932, L. G. Sorden, county agricultural agent for Oneida County, met with executives from the local paper mill to discuss building a museum to memorialize the logging industry that had once dominated the area. The museum was built that year on land adjacent to the Rhinelander Paper Company. In the 1950s, when Highway 17 was widened and the paper mill wanted to expand its operations, the museum was moved to its present site in Pioneer Park in Rhinelander. The trees removed during the highway reconstruction were used to build the first buildings at the new location for the museum. Builders used their memories of logging camp buildings to construct the bunkhouse, kitchen, and dining hall.[1]

This steam hauler is among the collections of the Rhinelander Pioneer Park Historical Complex Logging Museum. PHOTO © STEVE APPS

Today, the museum includes a collection of artifacts relating to early Wisconsin loggers, including peavies, pike poles, cant hooks, and crosscut saws, as well as photographs depicting life in Wisconsin logging camps. The museum features a replica logging camp bunkhouse, a cook shanty, and a blacksmith shop. Early equipment on display includes a road icer machine, a steam hauler, and the eighty-thousand-pound Thunder Lake steam engine that ran on narrow-gauge railroads hauling logs. For more information, visit http://rhinelander-resorts.com/loggingmus/logging.htm.

CAMP FIVE LOGGING MUSEUM

Camp Five was the fifth logging camp of the Connor Lumber and Land Company in Laona and operated in the late 1890s. In 1914, Camp Five became a farm, raising meat, produce, and draft horses for the Connor lumber camps. Gordon R. Connor and Mary Roddis Connor founded the Camp Five Museum in 1969 "as a gift to Wisconsin and the Nation in Honor of the U.S. Bi-Centennial in 1976." The farmland surrounding Camp Five became Heritage Acres in 1982 and is now owned by Mary

Connor's daughter Catherine Connor Dellin. Camp Five is a nonprofit foundation run by a board of directors.[2] The mission of the museum is to provide educational opportunities for visitors to learn about Wisconsin forestry history and the management of present-day forests. In 1996, it was listed on the National Register of Historic Places.

Visitors to Camp Five arrive at the museum on the Laona and Northern Railroad, using a "4-spot" steam locomotive built in 1916. Visitors board the Lumberjack Steam Train at the 1880s Soo Line Depot, located a quarter mile west of the junction of Highway 8 and Highway 32. Arriving at the site of the old logging camps and former camp farm, visitors can see several of the old buildings that were a part of the Connor Lumber and Land Company Farm, including the animal barn and blacksmith shop. For more information visit www.camp5museum.org.

PAUL BUNYAN LOGGING CAMP MUSEUM

Located in Eau Claire's Carson Park, this museum dates back to 1931 when Dr. Roy E. Mitchell and Dr. E. C. Murphy decided that the Chippewa Valley's logging history should be preserved. Using white pine donated from Mitchell's farm, employees of the city built the first buildings. The museum opened in 1934 and was donated to the city in 1936. Today the museum includes several buildings depicting early days in area logging camps. For more information, visit www.paulbunyancamp.org/about_us.phtml.

WABENO LOGGING MUSEUM

Located on Branch Street (Highway 32) in Wabeno, the museum features artifacts from the early logging days in the area. For more information, visit http://friendsofwabeno.org/historical_attractions.html.

MARINETTE COUNTY HISTORICAL LOGGING MUSEUM

Located on Stephenson Island in the city of Marinette, the Marinette County Historical Museum features logging equipment from the early days of logging in the Northwoods. For more information, visit www .marinette.wi.us/270/Museums.

FORESTRY AND WOODLANDS ORGANIZATIONS

NATIONAL FOREST PRODUCTS LABORATORY

In the early 1900s, the US Forest Service wanted to establish a site for researching the physical properties of wood. After reviewing several research universities as possible sites, Chief Forester Gifford Pinchot selected the University of Wisconsin–Madison. On October 1, 1909, the Forest Products Laboratory began operations, and the official dedication ceremony took place on June 4, 1910.

The laboratory was organized into four research divisions: wood preservation, wood chemistry, timber tests, and wood technology. Not long after it began operations, four additional research areas were added: pulp and paper, wood distillation, pathology, and engineering.

During World War I and World War II, the laboratory made several contributions to the war effort, including research on wood used in airplane construction, box and packaging materials, and charcoal used in gas masks. Other studies resulted in reducing demand for railroad ties by 75 percent through research on wood preservatives, increasing average lumber yield per log from 25 percent to 60 percent, and designing and constructing the nation's first prefabricated home. With cooperative research programs with nearly every state in the nation, the Forest Products Laboratory in Madison is the nation's only federally funded wood utilization research laboratory.[1]

Wisconsin Woodland Owners Association

About 12 million of Wisconsin's 17 million acres of forestland is held in private ownership. The Wisconsin Woodland Owners Association (WWOA) grew out of a 1953 forestry conference in Milwaukee that cited the need for an organization of private forestland owners. In 1976, the Wisconsin Department of Natural Resources applied for a US Forest Service grant that resulted in a partnership with the University of Wisconsin–Madison to form the state's first organization for private woodland owners. At its first meeting, on June 7, 1979, the organization developed its vision and goals, which include developing a public appreciation for the value of Wisconsin woodlands and fostering and encouraging the wise use and management of Wisconsin's woodlands.

The organization publishes a quarterly publication, *Wisconsin Woodlands*, and holds statewide and regional educational workshops and tours designed to keep forestland owners up to date with best management practices for their woodlots. The organization also keeps state legislators apprised of woodland issues, as well as voicing its perspective on pending legislation related to private woodland owners. The organization has thirteen local chapters, each with its own chapter chair and local programs.[2]

As of 2017, WWOA has 1,700 members. Some of the group's notable accomplishments in recent years include:

- Receiving a grant to create *My Land Handbook*, designed to help landowners share their forest management records with the next generation.

- Increasing educational efforts to help woodland owners "understand how their decisions impact the future of their woods, whether it be deer browse, emerald ash borer, invasive plants, climate change or the decline of Wisconsin DNR services and the need to hire professional foresters to assist them."

- Offering a Women of the WWOA program "to help women learn about caring for their woodlands."

- Establishing a Forestry Leader Scholarship at the University of Wisconsin–Stevens Point for future foresters.

- Representing private woodland owners on such issues as pro-
  posed changes in the Managed Forest Law program and the
  sunsetting of the forestry mill tax.[3]

FOREST HISTORY ASSOCIATION OF WISCONSIN

Organized in 1975, the Forest History Association of Wisconsin began
with the stated purpose of "stimulating an interest in the discovery and
preservation of the record in old journals, aging photographs, and in the
fading recollections of those who took their youth into the vast and shad-
owy depths of the Wisconsin pinery." Frank Fixmer, a longtime secretary
of the group, said, "Our basic objective is to educate the general public on
the contributions the forest industry has made to the social and economic
development in this state."[4]

In 2017, the organization had about 150 members. The organization
publishes a monthly electronic newsletter, *Woodchips*, and a quarterly
print newsletter, *Chips and Sawdust*. Its members collect publications
related to logging history and forestry that are held at the University of
Wisconsin–Stevens Point Archives.

WISCONSIN COUNCIL ON FORESTRY

The Wisconsin Council on Forestry has operated since 1981 by executive
order during Governor Lee Dreyfus's tenure; Wisconsin state statute 26.02
formalized the council's existence in 2002, with the following mandate:
"The council on forestry shall advise the governor, the legislature, the
department of natural resources, and other state agencies, as determined
to be appropriate by the council, on all of the following topics as they affect forests located in this state. . . . The council on forestry shall prepare
a biennial report on the status of the state's forest resources and forestry
industry."[5] The council consists of twenty governor-appointed members
representing the forestry industry and related interests; members include
the chief state forester, a state assembly representative, and a state senate
representative plus industry, private, and public forest representatives.

GREAT LAKES TIMBER PROFESSIONALS ASSOCIATION

For more than seventy years, the Great Lakes Timber Professionals Association has provided leadership for Michigan's and Wisconsin's forest products industry. It is a nonprofit organization whose purpose "is to practice, promote and enhance the forest products industry through sustainable forestry practices to protect the forests' renewable resources for years to come."[6] The organization sponsors logging expositions, works on legislative issues, conducts educational forums, and publishes the monthly *Great Lakes TPA*.

NOTES

Introduction

1. Robert F. Fries, *Empire in Pine: The Story of Lumbering in Wisconsin, 1830–1900* (Madison: State Historical Society of Wisconsin, 1951), 3.

Chapter 1

1. Mark Wyman, *The Wisconsin Frontier* (Bloomington: Indiana University Press, 1998), 22–23.
2. Mary Dopp, "Geographical Influences in the Development of Wisconsin," *Bulletin of the American Geographical Society* 45, no. 10 (1913): 736–49.
3. Forest W. Stearns, "History of the Lake States Forests: Natural and Human Impacts," in *Lake States Regional Forest Resources Assessment: Technical Papers*, ed. J. Michael Vasievich and Henry H. Webster (St. Paul, MN: US Department of Agriculture, Forest Service, North Central Forest Experiment Station, 1997), 8–29.
4. Native Languages of the Americas, "Native American Pine Tree Mythology," no date, www.native-languages.org/pine-tree.htm.
5. Wisconsin Department of Health Services, "American Indians in Wisconsin" (September 10, 2018), www.dhs.wisconsin.gov/minority-health/population/amind-pophistory.htm.
6. Gerald W. Williams, *References on the American Indian Use of Fire in Ecosystems* (Washington, DC: USDA Forest Service, 2003), 4.
7. Patty Loew, *Native People of Wisconsin* (Madison: Wisconsin Historical Society Press, 2015), 9–10.
8. Alice E. Smith, *From Exploration to Statehood*, The History of Wisconsin, vol. 1 (Madison: State Historical Society of Wisconsin, 1973), 499–501.
9. Erika Janik, *A Short History of Wisconsin* (Madison: Wisconsin Historical Society Press, 2010), 20–21, 25.
10. Robert F. Fries, *Empire in Pine: The Story of Lumbering in Wisconsin, 1830–1900* (Madison: State Historical Society of Wisconsin, 1951), 4.
11. Malcolm Rosholt, *The Wisconsin Logging Book, 1839–1939* (Rosholt, WI: Rosholt House, 1980), 5.
12. Frederick Hale, *Swedes in Wisconsin* (Madison: Wisconsin Historical Society Press, 2002), 60.
13. Fries, *Empire in Pine*, p. 11.
14. Portage County Historical Society, "Portage County Time Line 1827 thru 1849," no date, www.pchswi.org/archives/timeline.html.

15. Fries, *Empire in Pine*, p. 11.

16. C. E. Twining, "Plunder and Progress: The Lumbering Industry in Perspective," *Wisconsin Magazine of History* 47, no. 2 (Winter 1963): 116–24.

Chapter 2

1. Ralph W. Hidy, Frank Ernest Hill, and Allan Nevins, *Timber and Men: The Weyerhaeuser Story* (New York: Macmillan, 1963), 15.

2. Filbert Roth, *On the Forestry Conditions of Northern Wisconsin*, Bulletin No. 1, Economic Series No. 1 (Madison: Wisconsin Geological and Nature History Survey, 1898), 18.

3. Robert C. Nesbit and William F. Thompson, *Wisconsin: A History*, 2nd ed. (Madison: University of Wisconsin Press, 1973, 1989), 297.

4. Alice E. Smith, *From Exploration to Statehood*, The History of Wisconsin, vol. 1 (Madison: State Historical Society of Wisconsin, 1973), 508–10; Rodney C. Loehr, "Franklin Steele, Frontier Businessman," *Minnesota History* 27, no. 4 (1946): 309–18, http://collections.mnhs.org/MNHistory Magazine/articles/27/v27i04p309-318.pdf.

5. Robert F. Fries, *Empire in Pine: The Story of Lumbering in Wisconsin, 1830–1900* (Madison: State Historical Society of Wisconsin, 1951), 12.

6. Fries, *Empire in Pine*, 13.

7. Richard N. Current, *The Civil War Era, 1848–1873*, The History of Wisconsin, vol. 2 (Madison: State Historical Society of Wisconsin, 1976), 456.

8. Frederick Merk, *Economic History of Wisconsin during the Civil War Decade* (Madison: State Historical Society of Wisconsin, 1916), 62.

9. Current, *The Civil War Era*, 379.

10. Merk, *Economic History of Wisconsin*, 64–65.

11. Joseph Schafer, *The History of Agriculture in Wisconsin* (Madison: State Historical Society of Wisconsin, 1922), 132–33.

12. Wisconsin Historical Society, "Logging: The Industry That Changed the State," no date, www.wisconsinhistory.org/Records/Article/CS409.

13. Wisconsin State Legislature, General Laws, chap. 83, §§ 1–15 (March 22, 1861), https://docs.legis.wisconsin.gov/1861/related/acts/83.pdf.

14. Wisconsin State Legislature, General Laws, chap. 209, §§ 1–3 (April 17, 1863), https://docs.legis.wisconsin.gov/1863/related/acts/209.pdf; Wisconsin State Legislature, General Laws, chap. 74, §§ 1–4 (March 6, 1869), https://docs.legis.wisconsin.gov/1869/related/acts/74.pdf.

15. Merk, *Economic History of Wisconsin*, 65.

16. Lizzie Rice Johnstone, *A Story of Pittsfield and Suamico* (De Pere, WI: Kuypers Publishing, 1928), 89.

17. Mary Dopp, "Geographical Influences in the Development of Wisconsin," *Bulletin of the American Geographical Society* 45, no. 10 (1913): 736–49.

18. H. E. Cole, "Early Knowledge of the Dells of the Wisconsin," *Wisconsin Magazine of History* 5, no. 2 (December 1921): 205–6.

19. Wm. Carson, "The First Mills of the Red Cedar," *Eau Claire Leader*, March 8, 1916.

20. Richard D. Durbin, *The Wisconsin River: An Odyssey through Time and Space* (Cross Plains, WI: Spring Freshet Press, 1997), 21; Hidy, Hill, and Nevins, *Timber and Men*, 21–22.

21. Dopp, "Geographical Influences," 736–49.

22. Dopp, 736–49.

23. Johnstone, *A Story of Pittsfield and Suamico*, 89–107.

24. Unknown author, "White Pine School District, No. 2, Town of Suamico" (unpublished manuscript, no date). Submitted by Shirley Posey, Suamico, WI.

25. Johnstone, *A Story of Pittsfield and Suamico*, 89–107.

26. John D. Buenker, *The Progressive Era, 1893–1914*, The History of Wisconsin, vol. 4 (Madison: State Historical Society of Wisconsin, 1976), 89.

27. Fries, *Empire in Pine*, 244.

28. Merk, *Economic History of Wisconsin*, 77–78.

29. Merk, 78.

30. Fries, *Empire in Pine*, 19.

Chapter 3

1. Jerry Apps, *Wisconsin Agriculture: A History* (Madison: Wisconsin Historical Society Press, 2015), 80; Paul Wallace Gates, *The Wisconsin Pine Lands of Cornell University: A Study in Land Policy and Absentee Ownership* (Ithaca, NY: Cornell University Press), 1943.

2. Robert F. Fries, *Empire in Pine: The Story of Lumbering in Wisconsin, 1830–1900* (Madison: State Historical Society of Wisconsin, 1951), 168, 170.

3. Fries, *Empire in Pine*, 168, 170.

4. John Emmett Nelligan, *A White Pine Empire: The Life of a Lumberman* (St. Cloud, MN: North Star Press, 1969), 49–54.

5. Martin Page, "The Days in the 50's," *Eau Claire Leader*, February 23, 1911.

6. Robert C. Nesbit, *Urbanization and Industrialization, 1873-1893*, The History of Wisconsin, vol. 3 (Madison: State Historical Society of Wisconsin, 1985), 62.

7. Nelligan, *A White Pine Empire*, 55–56.

8. Nelligan, 56–57.

9. Mark Wyman, *The Wisconsin Frontier* (Bloomington: Indiana University Press, 1998), 253.

10. Wyman, *The Wisconsin Frontier*, 253.

11. L. Barnum, "A Logging Camp," *Fennimore Times*, April 26, 1921.

12. Thos. McBean, "The Lumber Camps of Long Ago," *Chippewa Falls Independent*, January 14, 1915.

13. Malcolm Rosholt, *The Wisconsin Logging Book, 1839–1939* (Rosholt, WI: Rosholt House, 1980), 84–85.

14. Frederick Merk, *Economic History of Wisconsin during the Civil War Decade* (Madison: State Historical Society of Wisconsin, 1916), 66–67.

15. L. G. Sorden and Jacque Vallier, *Lumberjack Lingo* (Minocqua, WI: North Word, 1986), 117.

16. Frank E. Cummings, "Confessions of a Camp Cook," *Eau Claire Leader*, March 15, 1916.

17. Michael Edmonds, *Out of the Northwoods: The Many Lives of Paul Bunyan* (Madison: Wisconsin Historical Society Press, 2009), 35–36.

18. Page, "The Days in the 50s."

19. Paul Bunyan Logging Camp Museum, "What Was a Logging Camp Like?" no date, www.paulbunyancamp.org/history_of_logging.phtml; Fries, *Empire in Pine*, 27–28.

20. Charles C. Hamilton, *The Northwoods Journal of Charles C. Hamilton: An Englishman in Wisconsin's Lumber Camps, 1892–93*, ed. Mary Hamilton Burns (Rudolph, WI: River City Memoirs, 1992), 15.

21. Letters used by permission of Ray Clark. The letters appeared with others in Ray Clark, "Dear Father and Mother," *Voyageur* 16, no. 2 (Winter/Spring, 2000): 47–50.

Chapter 4

1. Robert F. Fries, *Empire in Pine: The Story of Lumbering in Wisconsin, 1830–1900* (Madison: Wisconsin Historical Society Press, 1951), 31–32.

2. Mark Wyman, *The Wisconsin Frontier* (Bloomington: Indiana University Press, 1998), 257.

3. Frank Aldridge, "Old-Timer Recounts Changes in Wisconsin's Logging Industry," *Antigo Journal*, December 21, 1923.

4. L. G. Sorden and Jacque Vallier, *Lumberjack Lingo* (Minocqua, WI: North Word, 1986), 139.

5. Frank E. Cummings, "Confessions of a Camp Cook," *Eau Claire Leader*, March 15, 1916.

6. Cummings, "Confessions of a Camp Cook."

7. Dell Chase, "Dell Chase: Cornell, Wisconsin," *American Life Histories: Manuscripts from the Federal Writers' Project, 1936 to 1940 Collection* (Washington, DC: Library of Congress, American Memory Archive, 1998 [digitized]), www.loc.gov/item/wpalh002898/.

8. Iva Trotier, "She Cooked While They Cut Timber," Community Brochure, *Rhinelander Daily News*, March 1976.

9. Thos. McBean, "The Lumber Camps of Long Ago," *Chippewa Falls Independent*, January 14, 1915.

10. Malcolm Rosholt, *The Wisconsin Logging Book, 1839–1939* (Rosholt, WI: Rosholt House, 1980), 96.

11. McBean, "The Lumber Camps."

12. William Alft, "History of Logging Era on Wolf River," *Antigo Journal*, June 7, 1932.

13. Martin Page, "The Days in the 50's," *Eau Claire Leader*, February 23, 1918.

14. "Lumbering in Chippewa Valley," *Daily Telegram* (Eau Claire, WI), February 2, 1916.

15. Rosholt, *The Wisconsin Logging Book*, 83.

16. Sorden and Vallier, *Lumberjack Lingo*, 33.

17. Sorden and Vallier, 161.

18. Rosholt, *The Wisconsin Logging Book*, 83.

19. Rosholt, 100.

20. Kurt Kortenhof, "The Living Legend of Rhinelander's Hodag," *Hodag Press*, no date, www.hodagpress.com/about.htm.

Chapter 5

1. Malcolm Rosholt, *The Wisconsin Logging Book, 1839–1939* (Rosholt, WI: Rosholt House, 1980), 119.

2. John Emmett Nelligan, *A White Pine Empire: The Life of a Lumberman* (St. Cloud, MN: North Star Press, 1969), 133.

3. Frederick Merk, *Economic History of Wisconsin during the Civil War Decade* (Madison: State Historical Society of Wisconsin, 1916), 67.

4. Rosholt, *The Wisconsin Logging Book*, 132.

5. Nelligan, *A White Pine Empire*, 134.

6. Rosholt, *The Wisconsin Logging Book*, 131–32.

7. Mark Wyman, *The Wisconsin Frontier* (Bloomington: Indiana University Press, 1998), 260–61.

8. Robert F. Fries, *Empire in Pine: The Story of Lumbering in Wisconsin, 1830–1900* (Madison: State Historical Society of Wisconsin, 1951), 45; Peavey Manufacturing Company, "History of the Peavey," http://peaveymfg.com/history.

9. William Alft, "History of Logging Era on Wolf River," *Antigo Journal*, June 7, 1932.

10. Jerome Kaczmarek, "Saga of a River Pilot," Portage County Historical Society, no date, www.pchswi.org/archives/bios/antonkawleski.html.

11. Rosholt, *The Wisconsin Logging Book*, 128.

12. Alft, "History of Logging Era."

13. Rosholt, *The Wisconsin Logging Book*, 120.

14. Alft, "History of Logging Era."

15. Kaczmarek, "Saga of a River Pilot."

16. Fries, *Empire in Pine*, 40.

17. Wisconsin State Legislature, General Laws, chap. 83, §§ 1–15 (March 22, 1861), https://docs.legis.wisconsin.gov/1861/related/acts/83.pdf.

18. Fries, *Empire in Pine*, 39.

19. Merk, *Economic History of Wisconsin*, 68.

20. L. G. Sorden and Jacque Vallier, *Lumberjack Lingo* (Minocqua, WI: North Word, 1986), 89.

21. Sara Witter Connor, personal correspondence, May 16, 2018.

22. Rosholt, *The Wisconsin Logging Book*, 129, 182.

23. Rosholt, 149.

24. Fries, *Empire in Pine*, 55.

25. Fries, 55.

26. John O. Anfinson, *The River We Have Wrought* (Minneapolis: University of Minnesota Press, 2003), 110, 179–85.

27. Mary Dopp, "Geographical Influences in the Development of Wisconsin," *Bulletin of the American Geographical Society* 45, no. 10 (1913): 739.

28. Dopp, "Geographical Influences," 739–40.

29. Ceylon Childs Lincoln, "Personal Experiences of a Wisconsin River Raftsman," *Proceedings of the State Historical Society of Wisconsin at the Fifty-Eighth Annual Meeting* (Madison: State Historical Society of Wisconsin, 1911), 184, 187–88.

30. Miriam Bennett, *Camera Man of the Dells* (unpublished manuscript, no date), pp. 36–43. Available at Mead Public Library, Wisconsin Rapids, WI.

31. Bennett, *Camera Man*, 36–43.

32. Fries, *Empire in Pine*, 49.

33. Richard D. Durbin, *The Wisconsin River: An Odyssey through Time and Space* (Cross Plains, WI: Spring Freshet Press, 1997), 45.

Chapter 6

1. Ralph W. Hidy, Frank Ernest Hill, and Allan Nevins, *Timber and Men: The Weyerhaeuser Story* (New York: Macmillan, 1963), 19.

2. Frederick Merk, *Economic History of Wisconsin during the Civil War Decade* (Madison: State Historical Society of Wisconsin, 1916), 75.

3. Hidy, Hill, and Nevins, *Timber and Men*, 3–9, 31–32.

4. Hidy, Hill, and Nevins, 3–9, 31–32.

5. Mark Wyman, *The Wisconsin Frontier* (Bloomington: Indiana University Press, 1998), 267.

6. Wisconsin Historical Society, "Weyerhaeuser, Frederick 1834–1914: Lumberman and Timber Mogul," no date, www.wisconsinhistory.org /Records/Article/CS1681.

7. Wyman, *The Wisconsin Frontier*, 272.

8. Wisconsin Historical Society, "Weyerhaeuser, Frederick."

9. Information about Knapp, Stout, and Company drawn from Dunn County Historical Society, "The Knapp Stout & Company," www.dunnhistory.org; H. R. Holand, "The Knapp, Stout & Co. Lumber Company," *Wisconsin Magazine of History* 3, no. 4 (June 1920): 469–70;. Robert F. Fries, *Empire in Pine: The Story of Lumbering in Wisconsin, 1830–1900* (Madison: State Historical Society of Wisconsin, 1951).

10. Fries, *Empire in Pine*, 127–28.

11. Information in the next three paragraphs about the Connor family's lumber enterprises drawn from Mary Roddis Connor, *A Century with Connor Timber* (Wausau, WI: Connor Forest Industries, 1972); Gordon P. Connor, personal correspondence, May 28, 2018; Sara Witter Connor, personal correspondence, May 3, 2018; "Connor Company Observes 100 Years, 1872–1972," *Forest Republican*, June 22, 1972; "Connor Mill," no date, www.laonahistory.com/ConnorMill.html; and "History of Laona" (digitized pages from *Golden Jubilee*, 1952), www.laonahistory.com/Laona HistoryJubilee.html.

12. Maple Flooring Manufacturers Association, Inc., "Class of 2008," no date, www.maplefloor.org/About-MFMA/MFMA-Hall-of-Fame/William -Duncan-Connor.aspx.

13. Details about Ingram's life are from W. F. Bailey, *History of Eau Claire, Wisconsin, Past and Present: Including an Account of the Cities, Towns and Villages of the County* (Chicago: C. F. Cooper, 1914), 740–45.

14. University of Wisconsin Digital Collections, "UW La Crosse Steamboat Photographs," https://uwdc.library.wisc.edu/collections/lacrossesteam boat.

15. Long Lake (Wisconsin) Chamber of Commerce, "History of Long Lake," no date, http://longlakewisconsin.org/history.

16. Bailey, *History of Eau Claire*, 745.

17. Details about the Heinemanns drawn from Wisconsin Historical Society,

"Historial Essay: Heinemann, Benjamin 1850–1919," no date, www
.wisconsinhistory.org/Records/Article/CS8622.

18. Fries, *Empire in Pine*, 228.

19. Halford Erickson, *Ninth Biennial Report of Bureau of Labor and Industrial Statistics, 1898–1899*, State of Wisconsin (Madison, WI: Democrat Printing, 1901), 235–338.

20. Merk, *Economic History of Wisconsin*, 109.

21. Fries, *Empire in Pine*, 206.

Chapter 7

1. Frederick Merk, *Economic History of Wisconsin during the Civil War Decade* (Madison: State Historical Society of Wisconsin), 1916, 76.

2. James P. Leary, *Wisconsin Folklore* (Madison: University of Wisconsin Press, 1998), 371.

3. Robert F. Fries, *Empire in Pine: The Story of Lumbering in Wisconsin, 1830–1900* (Madison: Wisconsin Historical Society Press, 1951), 236–37.

4. Michael Edmonds, *Out of the Northwoods: The Many Lives of Paul Bunyan* (Madison: Wisconsin Historical Society Press, 2009), 47.

5. Randall Rohe, "Lumbering, Wisconsin's Northern Urban Frontier," in *Wisconsin Land and Life*, ed. Robert C. Ostergren and Thomas R. Vale (Madison: University of Wisconsin Press, 1997), 225–28.

6. John C. Hudson, "The Creation of Towns in Wisconsin," in Ostergren and Thomas, eds., *Wisconsin Land and Life*, 229.

7. History of Rhinelander throughout this section drawn from Rhinelander Logging Museum, Writers' Program of the Work Projects Administration in the State of Wisconsin, and Federal Art Project, *The Rhinelander Logging Museum* (Rhinelander, WI: Old Rhinelander), 1940, reprinted 2004.

8. George O. Jones, *History of Lincoln, Oneida and Vilas Counties Wisconsin* (Minneapolis and Winona, MN: H. C. Cooper Jr. and Co., 1924.)

9. History of Tomahawk drawn from Richard D. Durbin, *The Wisconsin River: An Odyssey through Time and Space* (Cross Plains, WI: Spring Freshet Press, 1997), 30–33.

10. History of Woodruff based on Marsha Schlecht Bast and Helen Schlezewske Schlecht, *A Woodruff Album: 1888–1988* (Woodruff, WI: Woodruff Centennial Committee, 1988), 15, 31.

11. Susan Armour, personal correspondence, May 23, 2017.

12. Details and quotes about Goodman drawn from Randall Rohe, "Goodman's Origin & Years as a Lumber Company Town," in *Goodman, Wisconsin,*

1908–2008: Centennial, a Historic Look at Our Community, ed. Bernie Draxler-Laurich, Joan Flannery, and Jack Gostisha (Goodman, WI: Goodman Centennial Committee, 2008).

Chapter 8
1. "Steam Engine," *UXL Encyclopedia of Science* at Encyclopedia.com, no date, www.encyclopedia.com/science-and-technology/technology /technology-terms-and-concepts/steam-engine.
2. Robert F. Fries, *Empire in Pine: The Story of Lumbering in Wisconsin, 1830–1900* (Madison: Wisconsin Historical Society Press, 1951), 55, 69–70.
3. Fries, *Empire in Pine*, 18–19.
4. Malcolm Rosholt, *The Wisconsin Logging Book, 1839–1939* (Rosholt, WI: Rosholt House, 1980), 223.
5. Chippewa Valley Museum, "Phoenix Log Hauler," no date, www.chippe pedia.org/Phoenix+Log+Hauler.
6. Rosholt, *The Wisconsin Logging Book*, 60.
7. George N. Harder, "Use of Log Hauler for Logging," *Chips and Sawdust* (newsletter of the Forest History Association of Wisconsin) (Summer/Fall 2016): 1.
8. Richard N. Current, *The Civil War Era, 1848–1873*, The History of Wisconsin, vol. 2, (Madison: State Historical Society of Wisconsin,1976), 35; History.com editors, "Manifest Destiny" (June 6, 2019), www.history.com /topics/westward-expansion/manifest-destiny.
9. Fries, *Empire in Pine*, 86.
10. Mary Roddis Connor, *A Century with Connor Timber* (Wausau, WI: Connor Forest Industries, 1972), 5.
11. John C. Hudson, "The Creation of Towns in Wisconsin," in *Wisconsin Land and Life*, ed. Robert C. Ostergren and Thomas R. Vale (Madison: University of Wisconsin Press, 1997), 207–11.
12. Sara Witter Connor, personal correspondence, May 3, 2018.
13. Sara Witter Connor, personal correspondence, May 16, 2018, and May 22, 2018.
14. Rosholt, *The Wisconsin Logging Book*, 67.
15. Rosholt, 67.
16. Robert Gough, *Farming the Cutover: A Social History of Northern Wisconsin, 1900–1940* (Lawrence: University Press of Kansas, 1997), 10–11.
17. Increase Allen Lapham, Joseph Gillett Knapp, and H. Crocker, *Report on the Disastrous Effect on the Destruction of Forest Trees Now Going On So Rapidly in the State of Wisconsin* (Madison: Atwood and Rublee, State Printer,

1867), 3; Vernon Carstensen, *Farms or Forests: Evolution of a State Land Policy for Northern Wisconsin, 1850–1932* (Madison: College of Agriculture, University of Wisconsin–Madison, 1958), 6–9.

18. Lapham, Knapp, and Crocker, *Report on the Disastrous Effect*, 3.

19. Lapham, Knapp, and Crocker, 100.

20. Fries, *Empire in Pine*, 239.

21. Randall Rohe, "Lumbering: Wisconsin's Northern Urban Frontier," in *Wisconsin Land and Life*, ed. Robert C. Ostergren and Thomas R. Vale (Madison: University of Wisconsin Press, 1997), 227–29.

22. Filbert Roth, *On the Forestry Conditions of Northern Wisconsin*, Bulletin No. 1, Economic Series No. 1 (Madison: Wisconsin Geological and Nature History Survey, 1898), 6, 54–55.

23. Randall E. Rohe, Stephen Miller, and Tim Eisele, eds., *One Hundred Years of Wisconsin Forestry: 1904–2004* (Black Earth, WI: Trails Media Group, 2004), 9.

24. Mark Wyman, *The Wisconsin Frontier* (Bloomington: Indiana University Press, 1998), 278.

25. Frederick Merk, *Economic History of Wisconsin during the Civil War Decade* (Madison: State Historical Society of Wisconsin, 1916), 110.

26. Fries, *Empire in Pine*, 240–41.

27. Joseph Schafer, *The History of Agriculture in Wisconsin* (Madison: State Historical Society of Wisconsin, 1922), 132–33.

28. Rohe, Miller, and Eisele, *One Hundred Years of Wisconsin Forestry*, 9.

29. Fries, *Empire in Pine*, 253.

30. Fries, 242–44.

Chapter 9

1. Robert Gough, *Farming the Cutover: A Social History of Northern Wisconsin, 1900–1940* (Lawrence: University Press of Kansas, 1997), 11.

2. C. Ford Runge, "Wisconsin's Northern Pineries: A Narrative Economic History," Working Paper WP02-8, Eighth Joint Conference on Food, Agriculture and the Environment, Red Cedar Lake, WI, August 2002, p. 28.

3. Gough, *Farming the Cutover*, 35.

4. William A. Henry, *Northern Wisconsin: A Handbook for the Home Seeker* (Madison, WI: Democrat Printing, 1896), 7.

5. Filbert Roth, *On the Forestry Conditions of Northern Wisconsin*, Bulletin No. 1, Economic Series No. 1 (Madison: Wisconsin Geological and Nature History Survey, 1898), 4–6.

6. Joseph Schafer, *A History of Agriculture in Wisconsin* (Madison: State Historical Society of Wisconsin, 1922), 145, 147.

7. Ralph W. Hidy, Frank Ernest Hill, and Allan Nevins, *Timber and Men: The Weyerhaeuser Story* (New York: Macmillan, 1963), 31.

8. Unknown author, "White Pine School District, No. 2., Town of Suamico" (unpublished manuscript, no date). Submitted by Shirley Posey, Suamico, WI.

9. Randall Rohe, "Goodman's Origin & Years as a Lumber Company Town," in *Goodman, Wisconsin: 1908–2008: Centennial, a Historic Look at Our Community*, ed. Bernie Draxler-Laurich, Joan Flannery, and Jack Gostisha (Goodman, WI: Goodman Centennial Committee, 2008), 24.

10. Fiftieth Congress, Session One, Chapter 999, September 10, 1888.

11. *Antigo Republican*, January 1, 1891.

12. Gough, *Farming the Cutover*, 40–41.

13. "Merrill Man Buys 13,000 Acres Near Michigan Boundary," *Rhinelander Daily News*, September 20, 1926, reprinted in *Chips and Sawdust* (newsletter of the Forest History Association of Wisconsin) (Spring/Summer 2017): 7.

14. Frank M. White, E. R. Jones, and University of Wisconsin, Agricultural Engineering Department, *Getting Rid of the Stumps* (Madison: University of Wisconsin Agricultural Experiment Station, no. 295, 1918), 23.

15. Mark Davis, "Getting Rid of the Stumps: Wisconsin's Land-Clearing Program—The Experience of the Northern Lake Country, 1900–1925," *Transactions of the Wisconsin Academy of Sciences, Arts and Letters* 84 (1996): 12.

16. "A Decade of County Agent Work," *Annual Report of the Agricultural Extension Service*, University of Wisconsin, Madison, Circular 142, February 1922, 28.

17. H. L. Russell and K. L. Hatch, "Demonstrations Convince," *Annual Report of the Agricultural Extension Service*, University of Wisconsin, Madison, Circular 126, March 1920, 28–29.

18. "A Decade of County Agent Work," 31.

19. Gough, *Farming the Cutover*, 117, 123.

20. Gough, 117, 123, 133.

Chapter 10

1. Filbert Roth, *On the Forestry Conditions of Northern Wisconsin*, Bulletin No. 1, Economic Series No. 1 (Madison: Wisconsin Geological and Nature History Survey, 1898), 20.

2. Laws of Wisconsin, Chapter 450, June 2, 1903.

3. Robert F. Fries, *Empire in Pine: The Story of Lumbering in Wisconsin, 1830–1900* (Madison: State Historical Society of Wisconsin, 1951), 250.

4. Wisconsin Conservation Hall of Fame, "Edward Merriam Griffith," no date, https://wchf.org/inductees/griffith.html.

5. Laws of Wisconsin, Chapter 264, May 27, 1905.

6. Jeremiah Auer, "A Slice of Nursery System History," *Wisconsin Natural Resources Magazine* (June 2011), https://dnr.wi.gov/wnrmag/2011/06/history.htm.

7. Wisconsin Conservation Hall of Fame, "Edward Merriam Griffith."

8. Randall E. Rohe, Stephen Miller, and Tim Eisele, eds., *One Hundred Years of Wisconsin Forestry: 1904–2004* (Black Earth, WI: Trails Media Group, 2004), 40–42.

9. Rohe, Miller, and Eisele, *One Hundred Years of Wisconsin Forestry*, 43–44.

10. Jeremiah J. Auer, "A Century of Tree Planting: Wisconsin's Forestry Nursery System," *Tree Planters' Notes* 54, no. 2 (2011): 23–29.

11. Wisconsin Department of Natural Resources, "Forest Tax Laws" (July 28, 2017), https://dnr.wi.gov/topic/forestlandowners/tax.html.

12. *Forestry in Wisconsin: A New Outlook*, Official Report of the Wisconsin Commercial Forestry Conference, Milwaukee, March 28–29, 1928 (Milwaukee, WI: H. L. Ashworth, 1928), i.

13. *Forestry in Wisconsin*, 171.

14. *Forestry in Wisconsin*, 171.

15. *Forestry in Wisconsin*, 171.

16. Auer, "A Slice of Nursery System History."

17. G. Graham Waite, "Land Use Controls and Recreation in Northern Wisconsin," *Marquette Law Review* 42 (Winter 1959): 275.

18. S. A. Witzel, *A History for the Period 1903–1975 of the Agricultural Engineering Department in the College of Agricultural and Life Sciences, University of Wisconsin–Madison* (unpublished manuscript, 1976), 2–3.

19. Witzel, "A History for the Period 1903–1975," 2–3.

20. Rohe, Miller, and Eisele, *One Hundred Years of Wisconsin Forestry*, 59; Forest W. Stearns, "History of the Lake States Forests: Natural and Human Impacts," in *Lake States Regional Forest Resources Assessment: Technical Papers*, ed. J. Michael Vasievich and Henry H. Webster, (St. Paul, MN: U.S. Department of Agriculture, Forest Service, North Central Forest Experiment Station, 1997) 8–29.

21. Laws of Wisconsin, Chapter 57, April 22, 1927.

22. Fred B. Trenk, *The County Forests of Wisconsin* (Madison: Wisconsin Conservation Department, 1938), 2; Wisconsin Department of Natural Resources, "County Forests" (January 20, 2017), https://dnr.wi.gov/topic/countyforests.

23. Wisconsin Department of Natural Resources, "Brule River State Forest:

History and Features" (June 13, 2019), https://dnr.wi.gov/topic/State
Forests/bruleRiver/history.html.

24. US Forest Service, "Chequamegon-Nicolet National Forest: History and
Culture," no date, https://www.fs.usda.gov/main/cnnf/learning/history
-culture.

25. Wisconsin State Legislature, 1927, Chapter 28.20.

26. Madison Metropolitan School District, "School Forests: Their Origin in
Wisconsin," no date, https://environment.madison.k12.wi.us/forest
/edwischf.htm.

27. *Madison Metropolitan School District School Forest Education Plan* (Madison,
WI: Madison Metropolitan School District, 2010), 5.

28. Auer, "A Slice of Nursery System History."

Epilogue

1. Stihl USA, "History," www.stihlusa.com/information/corporate/about-us
/stihl-company-history.

2. Fred Hengst, personal correspondence, November 7, 2017.

3. Katie Navarra, "Logging Equipment for Draft Horses," *Farming Magazine*
(March 10, 2016).

4. US Forest Service, "State and Private Forestry Fact Sheet, Wisconsin 2019"
(June 11, 2019), https://apps.fs.usda.gov/nicportal/temppdf/sfs/naweb
/wi_std.pdf.

5. United States Department of Agriculture, "Forests of Wisconsin, 2016,"
Resource Update FS108, February 2017.

6. Paul Fowler and Ron Tschida, "An Assessment of the Economic Contribu-
tion of Pulp, Paper and Converting to the State of Wisconsin," College of
Natural Resources, University of Wisconsin–Stevens Point, March 8, 2019.

7. Wisconsin Department of Natural Resources, "Value-added Wood Manufacturing Industry Survey Results" (May 1, 2019), https://forestrynews
.blogs.govdelivery.com/category/forest-products-news.

8. Fred Hengst, personal correspondence, November 7, 2017.

9. Wisconsin Department of Natural Resources, "Wisconsin Council on
Forestry."

10. Wisconsin Department of Natural Resources, "Wisconsin Forest Management Guidelines" (June 14, 2019), https://dnr.wi.gov/topic/forest
management/guidelines.html.

11. Steve Ring, personal correspondence, November 30, 2017.

12. Jenny Peek, "Climate Wisconsin 2050: New Resource Helps Communities
Adapt to Change," Nelson Institute for Environmental Studies (August 31,
2016), https://nelson.wisc.edu/news/story.php?story=2737; Steve Pomplun,

Richard Lathrop, Alison Coulson, and Elizabeth Katt-Reinders, "Managing Our Future: Getting Ahead of a Changing Climate," *Wisconsin Natural Resources Magazine* (February 2011).

13. Peek, "Climate Wisconsin 2050"; Pomplun et al., "Managing Our Future."

14. Wisconsin Division of Forestry and Wisconsin Department of Natural Resources, *Wisconsin Forest Products Industry* (Madison: Division of Forestry, Department of Natural Resources, 2017).

15. National Alliance of Forest Owners, "The Economic Impact of Privately-Owned Forests in the 32 Major Forested States" (April 2019), https://nafoalliance.org/wp-content/uploads/2018/11/Forest2Market_Economic _Impact_of_Privately-Owned_Forests_April2019.pdf.

16. Wisconsin Department of Tourism, "Tourism is an Economic Workhorse for Wisconsin," http://industry.travelwisconsin.com/research/economic -impact.

Appendix 1

1. Interview with Kerry Bloedorn, Coordinator, Pioneer Park Historical Complex Logging Museum, August 4, 2017.

2. Sara Witter Connor, personal correspondence, May 3, 2018.

Appendix 2

1. John W. Koning, *Forest Products Laboratory, 1910–2010: Celebrating a Century of Accomplishment* (Madison, WI: Forest Products Laboratory, 2010); University of Wisconsin, "US Forest Products Lab Centennial Oral History Project," 2008, https://uwdc.library.wisc.edu/collections/fplhist.

2. Randall E. Rohe, Stephen Miller, and Tim Eisele, eds., *One Hundred Years of Wisconsin Forestry: 1904–2004* (Black Earth, WI: Trails Media Group, 2004), 91–94; Wisconsin Woodland Owners Association, https://wisconsinwoodlands.org.

3. Nancy C. Bozek, personal correspondence, November 20, 2017.

4. Jim Lee, "Group Preserves History That Grew Wisconsin," *Wausau Daily Herald*, February 6, 1992.

5. Wisconsin State Legislature, Chapter 26, Protection of Forestland and Forest Productivity, 2602, https://docs.legis.wisconsin.gov/statutes /statutes/26/02.

6. Great Lakes Timber Professionals, www.gltpa.org/gltpa/default.asp.

BIBLIOGRAPHY

Anfinson, John O. *The River We Have Wrought*. Minneapolis: University of Minnesota Press, 2003.

Apps, Jerry. *Breweries of Wisconsin*. Madison: University of Wisconsin Press, 1992.

Apps, Jerry. *Wisconsin Agriculture: A History*. Madison: Wisconsin Historical Society, 2015.

Bailey, W. F. *History of Eau Claire, Wisconsin, Past and Present: Including an Account of the Cities, Towns and Villages of the County*. Chicago: C. F. Cooper, 1914.

Bast, Marsha Schlecht, and Helen Schlezewske Schlecht. *A Woodruff Album: 1888–1988*. Woodruff, WI: Woodruff Centennial Committee, 1988.

Bergland, Martha, and Paul G. Hayes. *Studying Wisconsin: The Life of Increase Lapham*. Madison: Wisconsin Historical Society Press, 2014.

Buenker, John D. *The Progressive Era, 1893–1914*. The History of Wisconsin, vol. 4. Madison: State Historical Society of Wisconsin, 1998.

Connor, Mary Roddis. *A Century with Connor Timber: Connor Forest Industries, 1872–1972*. Wausau, WI: Connor Forest Industries, 1972.

Connor, Sara Witter. *Wisconsin's Flying Trees in World War II*. Charleston, SC: History Press, 2014.

Current, Richard N. *The Civil War ERA, 1848–1873*. The History of Wisconsin, vol. 2. Madison: State Historical Society of Wisconsin, 1976.

Durbin, Richard D. *The Wisconsin River: An Odyssey through Time and Space*. Cross Plains, WI: Spring Freshet Press, 1997.

Edmonds, Michael. *Out of the Northwoods: The Many Lives of Paul Bunyan*. Madison: Wisconsin Historical Society Press, 2009.

Fowler, Verna. "The People Who Live with the Seasons." In *Wisconsin Indian Literature: Anthology of Native Voices*, edited by Kathleen Tigerman. Madison: University of Wisconsin Press, 2006.

Fries, Robert F. *Empire in Pine: The Story of Lumbering in Wisconsin, 1830–1900*. Madison: Wisconsin Historical Society Press, 1951.

Gates, Paul Wallace. *The Wisconsin Pine Lands of Cornell University: A Study in Land Policy and Absentee Ownership*. Ithaca, NY: Cornell University Press, 1943.

Glaab, Charles, and Lawrence H. Larsen. *Factories in the Valley: Neenah-Menasha, 1870–1915*. Madison: State Historical Society of Wisconsin, 1969.

Glad, Paul W. *War, a New Era, and Depression, 1914–1940*. The History of Wisconsin, vol. 5. Madison: State Historical Society of Wisconsin, 1990.

Gough, Robert. *Farming the Cutover: A Social History of Northern Wisconsin, 1900–1940*. Lawrence: University Press of Kansas, 1997.

Hale, Frederick. *Swedes in Wisconsin*. Madison: Wisconsin Historical Society Press, 2002.

Hamilton, Charles C. *The Northwoods Journal of Charles C. Hamilton: An Englishman in Wisconsin's Lumber Camps, 1892–93*. Edited by Mary Hamilton Burns. Rudolph, WI: River City Memoirs, 1992.

Henry, William A. *Northern WI: A Handbook for the Homeseeker*. Madison, WI: Democrat Printing Company, 1896.

Hidy, Ralph W., Frank Ernest Hill, and Allan Nevins. *Timber and Men: The Weyerhaeuser Story*. New York: Macmillan, 1963.

Hudson, John C. "The Creation of Towns in Wisconsin," In *Wisconsin Land and Life*. Edited by Robert C. Ostergren and Thomas R. Vale. Madison: University of Wisconsin Press, 1997.

Janik, Erika. *A Short History of Wisconsin*. Madison: Wisconsin Historical Society Press, 2010.

Johnstone, Lizzie Rice. *A Story of Pittsfield and Suamico*. De Pere, WI: Kuypers Publishing, 1928.

Kaysen, James. *The Railroads of Wisconsin, 1827–1937*. Boston: Railway and Locomotive Historical Society, 1937.

Kohlmeyer, Fred W. *Timber Roots: The Laird, Norton Story, 1855–1905*. Winona, MN: Winona County Historical Society, 1972.

Koning, John W. *Forest Products Laboratory, 1910–2010: Celebrating a Century of Accomplishment*. Madison, WI: Forest Products Laboratory, 2010.

Leary, James P. *Wisconsin Folklore*. Madison: University of Wisconsin Press, 1998.

Loew, Patty. *Native People of Wisconsin*. Madison: Wisconsin Historical Society Press, 2015.

Merk, Frederick. *Economic History of Wisconsin during the Civil War Decade*. Madison: State Historical Society of Wisconsin, 1916

Nelligan, John Emmett. *A White Pine Empire: The Life of a Lumberman*, St. Cloud, MN: North Star Press, 1969.

Nesbit, Robert C., and William F. Thompson. *Wisconsin: A History*, 2nd ed. Madison: University of Wisconsin Press, 1989.

Rath, Sara. *H. H. Bennett Photographer: His American Landscape*. Madison: University of Wisconsin Press, 2010.

Rohe, Randall E., Stephen Miller, and Tim Eisele, eds. *One Hundred Years of Wisconsin Forestry: 1904–2004*. Black Earth, WI: Trails Media Group, 2004.

Rohe, Randall E. "Goodman's Origin & Years as a Lumber Company Town." In *Goodman Wisconsin: 1908–2008*. Goodman, WI: Goodman Centennial Committee, 2008.

Rohe, Randall E. "Lumbering: Wisconsin's Northern Urban Frontier," *Wisconsin Land and Life*. Edited by in Robert C. Ostergren and Thomas R. Vale. Madison: University of Wisconsin Press, 1997.

Rosholt, Malcolm. *The Wisconsin Logging Book, 1839–1939*. Rosholt, WI: Rosholt House, 1980.

Schafer, Joseph. *The History of Agriculture in Wisconsin*. Madison: State Historical Society of Wisconsin, 1922.

Smith, Alice E. *From Exploration to Statehood*. The History of Wisconsin, vol. 1. Madison: Wisconsin Historical Society Press, 1973.

Sorden, L. G., and Jacque Vallier. *Lumberjack Lingo*. Minocqua, WI: North Word, 1986.

VandeBerg, Gale. "Land Clearing—Dynamite Blasting." In *And That's the Way It Was: 55 Stories of Farming and Rural Living in Wisconsin, 1880–1943*. Madison, WI: self-pub., 2001.

Wyman, Mark. *The Wisconsin Frontier*. Bloomington: Indiana University Press, 1998.

ACKNOWLEDGMENTS

As is true of all of my writing, many people helped me with this book, beginning with my wife, Ruth, who is first reader of all my material. I am blessed with a family of writers, journalists, and editors. My daughter, Susan, a published author, and my daughter-in-law, Natasha, a journalist and editor, helped with the project. My son Steve, a professional photographer, provided many of the contemporary photos. Kate Thompson, director of the Wisconsin Historical Society Press, assisted with the project from the early idea to the completed work. Without her help, the book likely would not have happened.

Sara Witter Connor, author, historian, and a member of the Connor lumber family, provided the history of her family's involvement in the lumber industry and read the entire manuscript in several drafts. She provided many corrections and helpful suggestions.

Michael Edmonds, former director of Programs and Outreach for the Wisconsin Historical Society and author of several books, including *Out of the Northwoods*, helped with a discussion of the Hodag and Paul Bunyan.

The following people provided information about logging or allowed me to interview them about various aspects of forest history: Ron Schuler, emeritus professor, Biological Systems Engineering, University of Wisconsin–Madison; Gale VandeBerg, former Wisconsin dean and director of Cooperative Extension; Jim Massey, former editor of *The Country Today*; Donald Schnitzler, Forest History Association of Wisconsin; Gordon P. Connor, president, Connor Timber Associates; Nancy Bozek, executive director, Wisconsin Woodland Owners Association; Steve Ring, past president, Wisconsin Woodland Owners; Fred Hengst, consulting forester; and Kerry Bloedorn, Pioneer Park Historical Complex Logging Museum, Rhinelander.

Numerous other people sent me stories and photos. I want to thank everyone who helped me with this project (though I no doubt am missing a few on this list): James Alf, Norm Anderson, Susan Armour, Jennifer Bahnaman, John Boettcher, Marjorie Boettcher, Kathy Borkowski, Robert Brown, Beverly Christ, Brent Christianson, Ray Clark, David Dueholm,

Don Greenwood, Sandy Grosnick, Craig Hayes, Angela Jensen, Lory Kohls, Joel Kroenke, Pete Morgan, Diane Mrkvicka, Dennis Nash, Nancy O'Kelly, Marjorie Olson, Julie Penshorn, Dawn Pophal, Shirley Posey, Bill Raaths, Rosemary Ryterski, Carol Clark Salm, Lynette Strasser, Judy Taylor, Arlene Vlies, Gordon and Joyce Walker, and Wanda Wiebusch.

INDEX

ABOUT THE AUTHOR

Jerry Apps is a former county extension agent and professor emeritus for the College of Agriculture and Life Sciences at the University of Wisconsin–Madison. Today he works as a rural historian, full-time writer, and creative writing instructor. Jerry is the author of more than forty fiction, non-fiction, and children's books with topics ranging from barns, one-room schools, cranberries, cucumbers, and cheese factories to farming with horses and the Civilian Conservation Corps. He and his wife, Ruth, have three grown children, seven grandchildren, and two great-grandchildren. They divide their time between their home in Madison and their farm, Roshara, in Waushara County.